Redistribution Of Wealth In America The New Civil War

Abraham Lincoln was an American Lawyer, politician, and statesman who served as the 16th President of the United States from 1861 until his assassination on April 15th, 1865 at The Petersen House, He was born on February 12, 1809 , in Larue County, Kentucky. He was married to Mary Todd Lincoln from 1842 until his death. They had four sons, Robert Todd, William Wallace, Edward Baker, and Thomas Tad Lincoln. Robert became a lawyer and politician like his famous father and was named by President Henry Harrison, as The Ambassador to The United Kingdon. Their other three sons died at an early age.

Redistribution Of Wealth In America The New Civil War

◦◦◦

MATTHEW CRUISE

ARPress

ILLUMINATING IDEAS,
EMPOWERING VOICES

ARPress
45 Dan Road Suite 36
Canton MA 02021
Hotline: 1(888) 821-0229
Fax: 1(508) 545-7580

Ordering Information:
Quantity Sales. Special discounts are available on quantity purchases by corporations, associations, and others. For details, contact the publisher at the address above.

Printed in the United States of America.

ISBN-13   Paperback   979-8-89330-534-0
               eBook   979-8-89330-535-7

Library of Congress Control Number: 2024901020

Table of Contents

"SOMEONE ONCE SAID "A WISHBONE WON'T DO, WHEN A BACKBONE IS NEEDED." AUTHOR UNKNOWN"

DEDICATION

To my lovely Wife Barbara Jackson-Cruise, who has stood by me and helped me pursue my dreams; and to my Lord and savior Jesus Christ.

ACKNOWLEDGMENT

I would like to acknowledge my agent, and cousin, Grace Adams (deceased), who always believed in me, and to my God who directs my path.

FOREWORD
By
Bob Bell

Bob is an entrepreneur, developer and civic leader. Having multiple business interests in Bakersfield; he understands the need for America to seek God and find truth in our founders' principles. He has been committed to forty years of service to those less fortunate than he; which has drawn him to seek first God's will and not rely on man's perspective. He is willing and driven to bring God back to where He belongs in Americas' future and is faithful in service to all he encounters. I am honored that my friend has taken time from his busy schedule to say a few words about our relationship and our vision.

I have known Matthew Cruise for over forty years; he is a fine Christian business man. His book "Redistribution of Wealth In America-And Beyond-The New Civil War," is a realistic workable approach to help solve this great nations economic and societal-woes, that has burdened the poor, and now threatens to annihilate the foundation that has made America the great country that it was, and return it to the position it has long held. His fresh and tested system of what he calls "circular economics," using "Micro Urban Farming." is the "shot in the arm that will go a long way in resetting America's future, without the help of government.

This effort must be made by and for the people. It is a sensible tried method of empowering the poor. It is a true to life, reenactment of what our founding fathers had in mind that all men are created equal and should have the right to life liberty and the pursuit of happiness. Through his God given talents he has tapped the very core of what makes our great country what can become again. I relish him as a friend, a Christian, and one of the most exciting new minds of where we are going in the twenty first century. It is most inspiring to know and share our thoughts on how we together can reshape America. It is a pleasure to see history unfolding before our very eyes as we move ahead.

MY CONFESSION

As I stated in my first book, Blood Bath In Jasper County Mississippi, my most difficult task was to decide upon the title of the book, not much has changed; when I talk to someone about this book, it takes a minute to tell them the title because its length; my other struggle is trying to write a story that involved life, in 2023, and skirt the very issues that drove me to write it in the first place. I promised myself that I would not write a hate book, or a blame book, but a conversational book; written in the same manner I use when I talk to a person or group. After almost completing it I realized two things, I had to do, the truth, and tell it as it happened. So I decided to simply report about events that has affected my life, and the personal stories and events of others who I interviewed or observed. Most of us are, for or against, a particular lifestyle, or belief, and that is alright. The people that you meet, will tell their story, that may help you see your story with a new set of rules, that will hopefully help you reset your course in life, no matter what your current circumstances may be. I must share a brief prelude to this book. If I do not, the book will not serve its intended purpose. If we can agree that we have been planted from the same seed (The Creation Story). If we can agree that all of us originated from the earth, and blossomed into what we call humans, and agree that the original seed, was created by God. If you believe there is a God, otherwise this book will only be "so many words" that can be used to validate your or my point of view. We are told that God formed man from the earth and gave him life, by breathing life into him. He then made woman by taking a rib from man and made woman. You can say they were the first family. Imagine if you will, a genealogy tree large enough to have every human who ever lived, on the tree of humanity. You and I are somewhere on that tree. I believe that a logical, honest person will agree, so far. So then, we are all cousins-at least. In order to grasp my point of view, when you see someone's leaf regardless of the many variances that seem to separate us, upon closer examination we can only see the effects and germination of the original seed. But underneath, we are all part of the root that came from one seed. Our story, yours and mine is continuing in this book.

Your Cousin,
Matthew

GETTYSBURG ADDRESS
BY
PRESIDENT ABRAHAM LINCOLN

Fourscore and seven years ago our fathers brought forth upon this continent a new nation, conceived in Liberty, and dedicated to the proposition that all men are created equal.

Now we are engaged in a great civil war, testing whether that nation or any nation so conceived and so dedicated, can long endure. We are met on a great battlefield of that war. We have come to dedicate a portion of that field as a final resting place of those who here gave their lives that, that nation might live. It is altogether fitting and proper that we should do this.

But, in a larger sense, we cannot dedicate-- we cannot consecrate-- we cannot hollow-- this ground. The brave men, living and dead, who struggled here, have consecrated it far above our power to add or detract. The world will little note, nor long remember what we say here, but it can never forget what they did here.

It is for us, the living, rather to be dedicated here to the unfinished work that they have thus far so nobly carried on. It is rather for us to be here dedicated to the great task remaining before us, - that from these honored dead we take increased devotion to the cause for which they have gave the last full measure of devotion, - that we here highly resolve that the dead shall not have died in vain, that the nation shall, under God, have a new birth of freedom, and that the government of the people, by the people, and for the people, shall not perish from the earth.

CHAPTER ONE
DEVIDED

Time and circumstances has brought about many changes since President Lincoln gave the aforementioned speech delivered at Gettysburg, Pennsylvania on November 19, 1863 have had far-reaching effects, in the development in this nation, both positive and negative. In America, we have fought a civil war, two world wars, a conflict with North Korea and numerous insurrections in the world. We have built a system of capitalism that is the envy of the world; we have traveled to the moon, landed on Mars, but we have fallen short of keeping the promise made by President Lincoln, and documented in the 14th amendment in the constitution. The promise to provide an equal opportunity for all members of this great country. The majority accuse those who have not shared in this promise, of being lazy, while purposely excluding many who were included in the original promise, including the original inhabitants of this country. I promise to try to address the facts that can be verified by history, and offer a tried and proven solution to eradicate poverty in America and beyond. Our government has not kept its promise; from a grassroots level, our government's promise accomplished no more than a doctor who make the correct diagnosis, but prescribe the wrong medicine to Cure a disease. Most people hate a dreamer, not real hate but they get confused when a person hold on to their dreams in spite of the current and historic circumstances. They ask, how can a person who is in the "same boat" as we, help solve our great economic and social problem? The ANSWER IS FAITH AND PRAYER. More directly the compassionate dream of Matthew Cruise, a welfare child, from a household lead by a mother who was a college graduate, and he with little education beyond high school, help solve the international problem of poverty. Well, here is how. I am and have always been

1

a dreamer; my dream is to better my spiritual, social and financial life, and in my family to the third generation better themselves. On August 3, 1983, I caught on to a new dream, a dream that required me to change my whole lifestyle, and my life. This dream included God and His desire for all men to experience true wealth, (a relationship with Him, and the gift of a loving relationship with each other). As we seek our individual dreams it is my prayer that they will include Him, and the implementation of ways and means for all men to fulfill and sustain the reality of their dreams. During my twenty years of honorable service in the US Army, that included three separate tours in Vietnam, for a total of thirty-three months, I learned how to use influence and assert power. I was assigned the "additional duty "as a Race- Relations/Drug Abuse, and Counseling Officer. I was able to sit with high-ranking Army officers, and see and hear first- hand, how they developed strategies to deal with volatile and emotional situations from within and without. I learned how to develop the art of strategic people-skills. I was able to be at ease in the presence of some of the most powerful men who were responsible for the welfare of hundreds of thousands of men and women in the military in Vietnam; and took from them a sense of self assurance that can only be learned through trial and error-and success and failure.

I have been married for the past forty–four years, to the same woman, Barbara Jackson-Cruise. I am involved in church and benevolent work in our local community, and in Kenya. This is the second book that I have written and if God wills it may not be the last. I was born at home in East Saint Louis, Illinois by a mid-wife who did not register my birth with the health department. My parents were not issued a birth certificate, a fact that later caused my first real dilemma. At seventeen, I wanted to get out of East Saint Louis, Illinois as fast as I could, in part because of the limited opportunities for young black or white men, with a high school education; and secondly, because I fell in love with the first girl who ever gave me the "time of day." I was only five feet six inches tall at the time, and she was four feet eleven inches. I was afraid that unless I married her, I would lose her, and possible look up to a future wife, (smile). I married my "first love" Kathryn Hicks-Cruise, in July 1954. She was a recent graduate from Lincoln

High School. We were married one month after I completed Basic Training on June 8th 1954. We had a total of four children, our first who died while sleeping in her crib.

Kathryn was never able to fully function without medication after the death of our girl, April Marie, in April of 1955; although we had three more lovely children, Matthew Jonathan Cruise, who is married to Marie Stancil of Bakersfield, California, Carmen Cruise, who was a Registered Nurse, here in Bakersfield, California who passed away in May of 2011, shortly after being elected to the presidency of the local nurses' union, and Michael, the smartest yet most troublesome of the three, who continues to be tormented by the fast street life, you will meet him later.

In 1972 I married a female Warrant Officer, who worked as an Army Intelligence Agent in Atlanta; we had a beautiful daughter, Evette Halcyon, and a son Kevin, who spent two tours in Iraq, and has since retired from the Army after twenty years of honorable service and now resides in Daegu, South Korea, and work with the U.S. Government as a GS-13. I thank him for his service

As I look back, although I retired from the Army after twenty years of contentious service, in 1974, except for the first three years after retirement, and three years after moving to California, I have always been the founder of an enterprise, by chance or design. I now believe that the Lord was preparing me for a "Red Sea" Experience, because I learned that "it takes a village". Little did I know that it would also take forty years for it to become a reality- Sound familiar?

It was common knowledge in Centerville, Illinois that a certain notary would certify a document that would allow young men to change their birthday without their parent's signature. I changed my birthday from May 1, 1936, the date that I thought I was born, to April 12, 1936, when in fact, I was born May 1, 1935; I did not discover this fact until I was almost sixty years old. I lied about my age because of my desperate need to go to the Army immediately. I had to try and better my circumstances in life – at all cost.

Most of the men in East Saint Louis, or Centerville, Illinois as it was called, worked until they were sixty- five, and many lived only a few years after retirement possibly because of the working environment where many of them worked; many of them died from respiratory diseases within five years after retirement. I wanted something better, and after learning that I could retire after twenty years of honorable service, I decided that the Army was the place for me. I will share some of my service experiences, and will highlight what I consider to be the things and the people, that help shape my life. Like most high school graduates, I enlisted as a private with the promise to attend airborne, and ranger school after basic and advanced individual training; little did I know, that you had to be a sergeant at the time, in order to attend ranger school. I could not prove that the promise, because it was not in writing. (Lesson number one, read the fine print).

I did complete airborne training as an artillery gunner and several years later, I applied and was accepted into Ranger School.

After three years I was still a private because I had not learned how and when, to keep my mouth shut, until a Sergeant Brown, from Memphis, Tennessee took me to "street college" by telling me the "oft" repeated phrase, "you can't buck city hall". During my third year, I tried out for the installation baseball team, at Fort Carson, Colorado. Our team won the All-Army Championship, and the Inter Service Championship; against all of the other services. In part, because we had George Altman, who later played for the Chicago Cubs, and later with my team, The St. Louis, Cardinals. Leon Wagner, who played for the San Francisco giants, St Louis Cardinals, Los Angeles Angels Cleveland Indians, and Chicago White Sox; Willie Kirkland, also a Giant outfielder, and played for nine seasons for San Francisco, Giants, Cleveland Indians, Baltimore Orioles and Washington Senators, and Charley Pride the first black famous country and western singer. I lost track of him, until 1962 when I heard that he had tried out for the New York Mets baseball team, during their first season in the major leagues

I played third base, and Mr. (Private), Billy Martin, was our coach. He was always on edge, but he really knew baseball. There was another player who was better, and had played double "A" ball prior to being drafted, but Billy told me that my love for the game, and my desire to win, made up for my lack of talent. I think he saw a little of himself in me. It really boosted my confidence, here I was with all of these great athletes and was accepted as part of the team.

After the championship, I was rewarded with a promotion to enlisted grade four and a special service job managing the driving range, with "Ole Sarge", Orville Moody, one of the greatest stickers of a golf ball that I had ever met. He met a local car dealer, (a Mr. Blackburn, I think), who was instrumental in backing his entry on the Professional Golf Tour.

Although he later won the U. S. Open in 1969; I am sure he would have won more except few knew that he was allergic to, of all things-grass. Even with this disability, he won a total of thirty-one tournaments. He was part Choctaw Indian and was very proud of it. His play on the Senior Golf Tour was more successful than his time on the regular tour. He never forgot our days at Fort Carson and sent me two sets of new clubs every few years. I re-enlisted in 1957, and was sent to Camp Casey, South Korea. It was there that I really began to come into my own, as a man, a father and a dreamer. My first son, Matthew J. was born in November 10th 1957, six months prior to my completion of my tour of duty.

I became a full-fledged "Jock" either playing or coaching basketball, football, or baseball, I had a natural ability to almost see things before they happened, and to design plays based on the possible outcome. I carried a seven-iron golf club with me to Korea, because it has always been my favorite club, in fact when I was a caddie at Grand Marias State Park in East Saint Louis, I would use that club for all the shots, driving, chipping, blasting out of the sand and putting. To say the least, it was my all in one club. I later won money with a trick shot that I learned from a sergeant while stationed at Fort McPherson, Georgia; I would bet anybody that I could escape from a sand trap on the first try, with a ball that was buried in the sand by stepping on it until all you could see was the apex of the ball. To this day, I can still do it-most of the time, but I now use a nine iron.

My biggest break during my Army service, came at Camp Casey, South Korea in 1957. I played football for the 7th Infantry Division and met General William F. Cunningham, and avid sports fan. His administrative aid was a Warrant Officer by the name of Thomas

Leggs who, believe it or not, was from my hometown, East Saint Louis, Illinois, (imagine, meeting a man from your hometown 6683 miles from your birthplace). One Sunday morning, a lean erect man came out where I was hitting golf balls on a rocky field. He told me that he had been watching me for a few Sundays, and asked if I ever missed a shot. I remembered an old joke that I told an Admiral while I was stationed in Hawaii in 1955; I was playing with a group at the Waialae-Kahala Country Club in Honolulu. I was a Private but my playing partner of the commanding general of the 25th Infantry Division located at Schofield Barracks; who always had a small bet on the game with another Navy Officer in charge of Pearl Harbor Naval Base. As usual, we won, and I made more money in three hours than I made the whole month.

I told the joke to my new admirer in Korea about the first Day that I played with three high-ranking officers; after hitting my drive over two hundred and fifty yards over a tall oak tree, that blocked entry into the left side of the fairway, my ball landed in the fairway about sixty yards from the green, the Admiral said "by God BOY', how did you learn to hit a golf ball like that"? I replied with a "straight face," and great anticipation, said, "Sir, a golf ball is the only thing white that I could hit in East Saint. Louis, without going to jail". This Very-erect officer and gentleman, after regaining his Composure, stood up from the rocky ground, he asked. with his face still red, if he could hit a few shots. I noticed that he that his grip and alignment was such that he could never hit a ball where he thought he was aiming. My teaching instinct kicked in and thankfully my tip helped him to improve his shot-a little, he was elated and for the next eight years, I went wherever the General Cunningham and Mr. Leggs except when I was assigned to Augsburg, Germany in October 1966, and after playing and coaching the Brigade baseball team I coached the local little league team in Augsburg, at the request of a Colonel Miller, who had a son playing for the little league team; we won the Bavarian Little League Title. I was selected to the coach the team from Bavaria in the German Championship held in Nurnberg, Germany, the most beautiful city that I had ever seen up to that time.

6

We lost the game in the finals to the home team. After eleven years of special duty the army cut back from full day special duty to a half day. I decided to try soldiering again. I rose to the rank of Sergeant First Class Enlisted Grade Seven. I wanted to become a Sergeant Major, the highest enlisted rank in the army, but I would have had to wait seven years to become eligible, which would be close to the time I had planned to retire.

Since I had made up my mind as a recruit that I would stay in service for twenty years, and at the suggestion of General Cunningham, I applied and was appointed to the rank of Chief Warrant Officer, after my second request, I was rejected on my first request, mainly due to my education level; even with the endorsement of a two-star general. On my second request my endorsement was written by a Colonel, (go figure). My specialty was in finance and administration. When the Vietnam conflict started I was assigned to a unit at Fort Lee, Virginia, for deployment in January 1967. I served three separate tours in Vietnam, because I was also trained as a race relations officer, and my turn around time was six months out of Vietnam, and eleven months in country, fighting the Viet Cong, and which-ever racial group that convinced themselves that I was a "uncle Tom" or a "raciest", (how do you like them little green apples)?

CHAPTER TWO

A NEW START A NEW HOPE

My new start after a turbulent marriage ended in divorce, began when I moved to Bakersfield, California in August 1978. After playing golf almost daily at the (now closed), Valley Grande Golf Course, my sister Freda Cruise Ray complained and insisted that I look for a job; in 1978, I was hired by the County of Kern to work for the local county hospital, as an administrator in charge of admissions, discharges, and collections of debts from the poor people most of whom could not afford to pay their medical bills, even though most could apply to the state for medical assistance, many would not follow through. It was if some viewed being poor as a "rite of passage," to not pay their bills. In most cases, the county required home owners who were denied, medical assistance to sign a lien that stipulated that the county, upon their death, and the death of their children, that the said property would belong to the County. I was never comfortable with this system, because, first, it reminded me of the requirement for fathers and husbands to move out of their homes in order for the mother and the wife to receive a welfare check, (In our family case, we received one hundred and seventy five dollars for nine boys and one girl); the other problem that I could not find the provision that allowed for the possibility that a home value could increase over time. That would require an adjustment to current value. In fact, I decided to look for something else when my wife's grandmother's property located at 1418 Virginia Avenue in Bakersfield, California, lien came to me for signature to be approved by voice vote by the county supervisors. I am not in love with money; nor do I have a burning desire to be wealthy, I am secure in the knowledge that wealth is only useful to help someone who cannot help themselves, many of whom are trapped in poverty with no way out. Currently there is a new movement among some billionaires to give all or most of their money away before they die, I suggest that they find grass-roots local organizations and "invest" in the future by funding entrepreneurial activities through organizations like the Grameen Bank, in the local community. It is clear to me that in spite of what others may say, I believe in America, but America has not figured out how to solve this great problem of the poor. We simply do not have enough people fishing, (thinking outside the box), instead they sit on the river bank, using the same bait, and getting the same results, while "waiting for THEIR ship to come in". Washington's methodology of treating the symptom and not the decease cannot and will not work.

While working at the hospital I was reintroduced to direct marketing, an industry that could be a major tool in helping thousands out of poverty today because of the system wealth by working together. I was introduced to t The Amway Corporation, short for The American Way, in December 1959 by a Major who attended Calvin College with Jay Van Andel, one of its co-owner. My wife decided to come to Fort Smith, Arkansas around the time that Central High School was desegregated, (bad timing), I had little or no money, and no place to live. When I told my Major about my problem, he suggested that I could join a new company called Amway. I found a room on 9th Street, owned by the Stephens family, after paying the rent of fifty dollars, I had fifty dollars left, I paid the distributor fee of thirty-one dollars leaving me with less than twenty dollars. The issue of race was volatile in Arkansas due to the situation in Little Rock. With and Red Sea situation I had to trust that God would provide a way for me. I started knocking on doors of white people on Saturdays, it was there that I crowned myself "the world's greatest salesman". On my second attempt, God allowed an angel to open her door. Her name was Mrs. Williams, her son was a pharmacist and there house was next to the drug store. I told her who I was, and the personal situation I had due to my wife coming unannounced to Fort Smith. I went on to tell her the little about the soap that I knew, and would like for her to buy a box for fourteen dollars and ninety-five cents, but with shipping cost I was three dollars and fifty cents short, and I needed to buy some for my son. She handed me twenty dollars, and asked me to return the following

Saturday. Upon my return with my first sale, I was more that shocked and afraid, when I was ushered into the back yard where twenty-five women were waiting for me. I left with six hundred dollars in orders. I stayed in touch with Mrs. White until she died in 1978. I went on to become one of the leading distributors in the company for seven years. I was later drawn back to the direct marketing industry by a very dynamic lady in the person of Mrs. Marione Wossne, who founded Marione Cosmetics. She appointed me to her corporate staff as the National Sales Director. It was my first taste of direct marketing at the national level even though I had success in Amway while stationed at Fort Chaffee, Arkansas years earlier, when Amway was just getting started. It was at this juncture that I remembered that years earlier I crowned myself "The World's Greatest Salesman", at a time when colored people were in the very act of integrating Central High School, it was a trying time all over the south and in Little Rock. Democratic Governor Orval Eugene Faubus, was bon January 7, 1910 (The same year my mother Letha Beets was born in Dumas, Arkansas, reminded people in the south that trouble was on the way, and soon colored boys would be marrying their daughters and having mixed babies.. It made Mrs. Williams act of love, also one of courage and love. During my stay with Mrs. Wossne Barbara and I made great sacrifices of money, time and energy to build a team all across the nation. While we were "team Building" in Illinois, Mrs. Wossne died suddenly from a heart attack. The business was never the same without her, and we knew that we could not hold it together and resigned. We were so disappointed and emotional because of our loss of the dynamic lady, we were not able to reach the success level that was right in our grasp.

I started a business In January 1990 called the California Gas Procurement Group (CGPG), with a young man from Jamaica by the name of Lawrence Watson, who was attending Bakersfield College on a track scholarship. We entered the natural gas industry marketing natural gas directly to customers transported by the customers' existing gas/transportation company. Although we were successful in marketing and attracting customers, and training other marketers, we were never able to obtain financing to purchase our product, even though our customer usage was over thirty million dollars a month.

Some people in the community looked upon us as a failure but we knew that we were winners even though we closed the business with no regrets, because we had temporarily given hope to many who had no hope, and it was another training ground in order to be prepared for our "Red Sea Experience."

During the same time, we tried the more traditional way of infiltrating the business vault; we were shocked to learn how much money it took to do business under the rules and regulations in the state of California. We found an Angel in the form of Mr. Glen Hierlmeier, a local leader, and then, president of Castle & Cooke, a large builder and developer in California and Hawaii. He was instrumental in helping us start a licensed commercial landscaping business. Our largest jobs were the landscaping extension of Memorial Hospital, Mondavi Apartments on Brimhall Road, and maintenance work for most of Castle and Cook's properties. We had eighty-three men and one woman on the maintenance payroll, and two women on the administrative staff.

Mr. Hierlmeier was replaced, I believe because of his direct involvement in the poor community, and we slowly began to be phased out and replaced by another local landscape contractor. We had to lay off seventy- five laborers that included six supervisors and our clerical staff.

During the construction boom we started a licensed cement and masonry business under the license of Johnny Luevano, who was a local contractor. Everybody made money even those who did not have a license. At the peak of the business, we had a staff of 87 employees half of whom were illegal immigrants, most of whom, later became citizens. We closed the business when the bottom fell out of the new home construction market. It seemed that every time we were at the brink of success, someone or something would deter us. The saving grace was we never lost hope in ourselves. It was about this time period that many black families were trying to find their ancestors. After my cousins Vernetta McGlaston, and Sherylita Mason Cruise began their search and found our great grand-father, James Cruise who lived in Paulding, Mississippi they shared their new-found information with me. Our family owe them a debt of gratitude for their work as well as our cousin Carl Brinkley, a retired police captain in East St Louis, who continues to probe the past in search for the Cruise/Foggy family history, surprisingly we have found that many of them had their own business, a fact that continues to this day.

I was blessed to travel to Kenya in 2008, with the help of three members of the Cypress church of Christ, in Cypress, California, Bill Carter, owner of Carter Automation located in Los Alamitos, California; Doctors Jessie Trice and his wife Jill, who succumbed a few years ago from a long-standing illness. Our first venture was a success, but the local administrators of our effort in Kenya at the time were dishonest, and stole a large sum of money from us. Everyone advised me to quit "because Africans can't be trusted."

In 2004, I met Melvin Thomas and his wife Kathy who lived in San Diego, California, while they were conducting a marriage retreat our local church. Within hours we were brothers for life. He was working with a group in Zimbabwe, trying to do the same thing that we were attempting to do in Kenya. As we continue our Kingdom Vision of helping people all over the world to better their physical and spiritual condition, for those who desired to know about Christ

In 2013 Melvin, my wife Barbara and I went to Kenya for three weeks to survey new possibilities that would help to empower the people in Sega, Kenya, and to organize a newly established church. Melvin baptized twenty-two people in one day, and we later taught two others who came to the Ongech family compound where we stayed. One man heard that we were in Sega and ran along the dirt road that we were traveling and asked if he could be baptized, there was a small ditch filled.

The first week we were confined to the compound, because the presidential election was taking place, and, and Melvin baptized him after making sure that he was aware of what and why he was being baptized. There was some fear of a replay of the post-election riots that occurred in the last presidential election. Thank God all went well, and we were able to visit the ten villages that we supported.

We made a three-year plan to dig a water well, purchase a van to transport people in the local area, start a poultry farm, and finally a gas station located on the main highway leading to Uganda. In the meantime, we continued to make loans to women; however, until recently the program was almost none existent.

It has taken us two years to finish the well, and we thank Dani Morill and the Vista church of church of Christ, in Vista California, who sent their entire offering on the first Sunday of September 2015, to Kenya to purchase mosquito nets and blankets for the widows and orphans.

We have the only drinking water in the city of Sega we named it "The Liquid of Life, and dedicated it to Dani's father and mother Charles and Bertar Morill. We continue to support the efforts by women and men to change their lives through growing crops to be sold locally and on the world market. We have been blessed beyond measure to have recently partnered with and organization in Nairobi, Kenya called Center For African Volunteers, founded by Mr. Josephat Moses Ochieng and and the International Institute For Research and Agricultural Development, LTD, (IIRAD Ltd., a for-profit corporation with offices in Nairobi, Kenya and Bakersfield, California. The principals are Mr. Ochieng and Mr. Matthew Cruise who lives in Bakersfield. Other stakeholders are U Can Grow located in Johannesburg, South Africa and Symbiosis AGx a manufacture of a bio stimulant located in South Bend, Indiana founded by Dan Pavich, an almost miracle product that will revolutionize how fruits and vegetable are grown world-wide. IIRAD has entered into a partnership with The Royal Seed Company of Nairobi, Kenya, to distribute AGx to their customer base of over one hundred thousand customers in five African countries.

CHAPTER THREE

THE TIE THAT BINDS US

Pull up From Poverty, Inc-Kenya (PUFP) and Pull Up From Poverty-America in Bakersfield, California partnered together to design a method to help eradicate poverty, both in America in Kenya and any third-world country. You will meet some of them on the boat named HUMANITY. In 2021 we added a for profit corporation, The International Institute for Research and Agricultural Development, LTD (IIRAD), In 2022 we formed The California Agricultural Biostimulant Cooperative, LLC, CABC, LLC, for the purpose of distributing Symbosis AGx, a biostimulant that will improve yield by sixteen percent, and decrease the use of pesticide and herbicide, as well as reducing irrigation requirements percent in the first year, and sixty-six percen every year thereafter. (A miracle growth product for sure, we will discuss miracles in a later chapter). As mentioned earlier, we are convinced that a person who has no hope, is on the road to losing their self-worth. Our program is designed to assist in curing the disease of feeling worthless; our treatment is a prescription of real hope, but not blind hope. The hope we offer translates into tangible action that can and will be measured. IIRAD with its principal owners Josephat Moses living in Nairobi, Kenya, and Matthew Cruise, of Bakersfield, Californiaa, has developed a system that will enable people from anywhere in the world to participate in micro cooperative farming. We want to introduce you to people that we have met, in order to help decide if you would like to join us. We want to introduce you to men and women who had little or no hope of ever changing their circumstances, or to achieve their fleeting dreams of a better life. They come from all walks of life, and parts of the world; they come from every racial and ethnic group, but most of them grew up in poor neighborhoods or rural third world countries. A large majority came from broken or single-parent homes, and have been disenfranchised from the main-stream of their society.

Many in our society have been enabled by the government through welfare, a system that leads to nowhere. Many are talented but have never had the opportunity or a platform to transform their lives and the lives of their families. This book is based on true life events in their lives, and the lives of those who join us on what we call The Boat, a place where all can be free. Here is our story. It is our desire that after reading this book you will look beyond your present circumstances and find not just hope but a tried method and a system to not only change your life, but to help others do the same thing. It is not how much you do at any one time, but how many times you do it. Although I heard a long time ago a true saying, "You don't have to be a big shot to accomplish big things, you just have to just keep on shooting." This truism was brought home when I read a book "The Compound Effect by Darren Hardy, who was the editor of Success Magazine; by taking his advice I was able to complete most of this book, by doing a little each day. It is our hope you will become part of our story. If we can do it anyone can. It is our hope and our prayer that this will be a new beginning for people who have not had anyone attempt to pull them up from poverty.

It is that same discipline that has given me direction in forming and actuating the program on a world-wide basis. At first, I felt unworthy and unprepared, to attempt such a task, not to mention the ability, or the funds necessary to manage this great effort. I felt like Moses must have felt when given his marching orders, to free the children of Israel from Egyptian bondage, and lead them over to the promise land.

I stopped worrying about who, what, when, where and how. I believed that my steps were being ordered by God. The answer was right there, it was the same answer that I received, when my doctor's and some of my "Job like friends" to not travel to Kenya the first time in 2008. My desire to help others, gave precedence over their objections. I received a faith answer that gave me a solid foundation of unswerving belief that compelled me to go, in spite of the objections. I was determined to go, in part because of my desire to locate my ancestors. My only clue was a saying that I often heard my grandfather use "Bonde la

Ufa" was Swahili for Rift Valley located in Kenya. After clearing customs, I met the welcoming party that I had never met before except through email and a few telephone calls. As often is the case with changing planes, my luggage did not arrive on the plane, and we had to remain in Nairobi until my luggage arrived from Turkey the following day. We stayed in a beautiful home not far from the airport, it was there that I first saw Erick Ongech, a brilliant young man who has ascended to the office of President of Pull Up From Poverty-Kenya. He is a major player in monitoring and development of loans, developing a major housing program in the villages creating jobs and entrepreneurial opportunities, heading an education foundation to pay for the education of cooperative member's children, treating many health issues, through the use of natural herbal medicine, to include teenage monstering of their futility period. All of these models are designed to be replicated and sustained by its members with little or no help from the government. In phase two we will approach the problem of fresh water and electricity off the grid. We thank God for Erick Ongech of Sega, Kenya, the President of Pull Up From Poverty, a local Non-Profit Organization (NGO), for directing the overall efforts of the organization.

TIMEOUT

Most of the remainder of this book is about people who are trying, or have escaped the misery of poverty. I have known some of them all of their lives, but most I have met in the past few years. They are from all walks of life and will tell their story in as much detail as they deem necessary. In my interviews, or actual experience of trying to help people change their lives, I have suffered a personal financial, and emotional issues that can cause you to lose hope; however, I have witnessed a gradual transformation in some of them, and a renewed hope that God will see us through. One major hurdle is hoping for a change in their lives without changing their life-style, or have fallen further down the road to nowhere, while continuing to blame the system without participating in the road to change and success. When I started our program in December 2015, I told myself that if I could change the life of one person, it would be a success. Guess what, there are numerous people who could be placed into the Pull Up From Poverty Hall of Fame.

As you read their stories, our prayer is that you will see the story of us, the story of you or, someone you may know. We believe that you will be inspired by their dreams, their aspirations, and their future and their successes. They are returning from the depths of a human condition that has enslaved them in a system of plantation living, a life where there appeared to be no way out.

I have been blessed to listen to their stories, and pray that their words will come alive in you as it has in some of them. I faithfully await to see the before and after, of the light that now shines off the mental plantation into a future of a positive self- worth, that will be a testimony of where they have come, and where they are going. And finally to understand that the success of their race to change must and can only start with them.

CHAPTER FOUR

PREPARATION FOR SUMMER

As you already know that as a young man, I began my business and sales experience out of desperation. I enlisted in the Army and after basic training married the first girl who ever gave me "the time of day. Since I was paid ninety-one dollars per month, and my new bride received an allotment of one hundred and thirty- seven dollars, times were hard. I was transferred to the 82d Airborne Division in order to receive additional pay for jumping out of airplanes called "hazardous duty pay", of an additional pay one hundred seventeen dollars per month, (during that time it was considered to be a lot of money). Although money was scarce, I was able to buy a house in my home town of East Saint Louis, Illinois. When I was fifteen, I worked for a white lady who hired me to cut her grass and trim her hedges.

She would always fix lunch for me and would ask me questions about my future. I told her that I wanted to own my own house although she seemed not to hear me, a few weeks later; she casually said, that when she retired and moved to Florida, I would be given first choice to buy her house. Whenever I came home on vacation, I would visit her. While on leave for thirty days prior to going to Korea in 1957, she told me that she was moving to Florida and wondered if I wanted to buy her house. I was stunned; I had over three thousand dollars that I had intended to use to buy a good used car for my wife, and before I knew what I was saying, I said yes. She was such a wonderful woman, she sold me the house for five thousand dollars, with five hundred dollars down. I owned my first house. I began my first business, when I returned from leave, I began jumping out of airplanes for people who paid me to jump for them. My fee was fifty dollars per jump; on a good month I would make five or six jumps for others, plus the occasion that I had to jump once every three months in order to receive my hazardous duty pay. went out for the football team at Fort Bragg, North Carolina and met a young soldier from Alabama who I could not read. When I asked how he was able to join the Army he replied that he had his twin brother take the test for him. We both made the team and I began to teach my new found friend the art of reading. I learned that I was a natural born teacher; in less than three months he was able to read at about the ninth-grade level. He later took the General Educational Test and obtained his high school diploma. After his discharge he attended college and at the age of thirty-two received a master's degree in Public Administration and became a tennis and football coach at a historically black college

During our stay in North Carolina, I started my second income earning venture. My football friend told me that his wife wanted to move to North Carolina and attend college but he could not afford to rent an apartment. I told him that I was in the process of buying at and his wife for two hundred dollars per month. I made a deal with my friend that if he would pay me two hundred dollars for first and last, he could live in my new house.

I went to the Veterans Administration and was approved to purchase a house at 103 Elliott Circle in Fayetteville, North Carolina. The house was less than a mile from Fayetteville State University (FSU). The house costs nine thousand nine hundred ninety-nine dollars, with a down payment of ninety nine dollars and ninety nine cent. The monthly payment was the same as the down payment. Thirty days later we moved in, which made me eligible to receive food ration allowance of thirty-five dollars-money was rolling in.

I always watched how people made money and with my God given talents, I looked for common needs and tried to fulfill them. It was through these many years of learning that I realized that I could help people pull themselves up from their current circumstances. It is through some the proceeds of my first book Blood Bath In Jasper County, Mississippi, and earnings from two business ventures in Kenya, have helped provide some funds to continue our work with women and men in Kenya and to start the same project in America. You will learn in a final chapter how I went "From Bankruptcy to a Billionaire in one year.

To date we have helped change the lives of approximately six hundred women and eight hundred orphans. It is now time that we bring our system to Bakersfield California, and then use the system of multiplying the seeds of love and hope. It is clear that the government with all of the best of intentions will never impact the "back-streets" and rural areas and of the ghettoes of America for several reasons. Institutional thinking, and lack of education of our youth, and for the men and women who are the head of the households; a lack of expectations of any positive input into their families or communities, compounded by the mental and physical blight experienced by our young men and women who inhabit rural southern America and our inner-city ghettoes and prisons of America.

The disenfranchised must have a vision that they can control their own destiny by establishing a common goal of success. In part they blame the government, but deep down in their soul, they know that much of their condition is from a lack of love of self, and others who are part of their lives.

Another obstacle that we must overcome is the culture of I want it now no matter what the cost, is a debt that cannot be paid with a check from city hall, our state houses, or from Washington. It must be done by using whatever is available to even the poorest among us, who have the audacity to kindle a renewed hope from within by joining together in what we call "the boat of life." Kern Family Island was poised to help those who desire to change their lives, we received initial help from the county of Kern, and the assistance of Mr. Lee Rangel, who was working in the county real estate division. We negotiated an agreement to lease a property owned by the county located at 1616 East California Avenue for one dollar per year for five years, because of many circumstance, some beyond our control and mistakes in judgement, the lease was terminated and sold to a man who has a automobile repair shop. We lost more than fifty thousand dollars in antiques and used clothes and household items that was being stored to start a thrift store. All of our records and files were thrown into the local trash dump. We will continue to treat the disease and not the symptom. We will require all of our coopt members to agree to submit to random drug and alcohol testing, members with a history of drug and alcohol abuse, must enroll in an out-patient- drug treatment program

The only thing that we have to communicate to my readers are words fueled by our passion, and our experiences of real life, day- to-day living. Unlike the musician, who use harmony to capture the ear and mind of their audience, authors must craft and serenade the emotion that make one word connect to the next in a rhythm that flows through the very fiber of the human experience.

There is little if any hope and dreams of a home, a car, an education for our children, and eventually a reasonable life-style after retirement for a great majority of our society. Those dreams have almost disappeared into the depths of hopelessness and despair.

There is no such animal as the "trickle down" effect that empowers the poor. The poor must be pulled out of poverty starting at the bottom rung of the socio-economic ladder, and be pulled to the rung above that is achieved by obtaining an equal footing. Their problem is their inability to reach the first rung, a basic education or whether a trade of the more traditional education.

All forms of government entitlement programs are simply enablers, because people who rely on this kind of life-style, have devalued and condemned not only themselves, but their children-to an existence no better than the person begging on the streets of America. They must be empowered, wherever we find them in life's cycle, whether it is in the spring, summer, fall, or winter of life, and begin to help them find hope, in order to live a productive life.

For most who are caught in this cultural, socio-economic web, government subsidy is the only lifeline that is thrown to the poor, as the rich berate their condition with wonderment, and no workable solution, causing the poor to totally lose sight of any aspirations that they may have had before this life sucking system became a way of life, finally ending in a deep abyss, where despair is the order of the day, and hope for their future is the last thing that die, and once buried, it is almost impossible to resurrect it.

Most poor Americans, black or white, have lost their trust in almost all branches of government. There is a total disconnect between what the leading experts, and "think tanks" who make their living by compiling data about the problem of poverty, while offering little if any plan to fix it. They are no more than a trained bird dog, who is proficient in pointing at the prey, but have little, or no participation in catching it, because they start pointing in several directions, like promises made but seldom kept.

In reality the government's fix is to tax the rich and save the middle class, many who own businesses who they believe will in turn hire the poor. Yet it seems that the government over regulate and tax the small to mid-sized business where it is almost impossible to make a profit even if they cut cost and increase productivity. The government does not have any other plan to help the poor. They present a long-range solution to educate the poor, most of whom, have not received a good basic education that will prepare them to complete high school, let alone to obtain a post high school degree.

People need is a fresh look outside the box to find ways to empower themselves to create their own methods of earning a living, to understand how "circular economics work, and practice it. I believe that the government should empower the people and not enable them, because it is not sustainable except to continue the pattern of dependence. The wealthy continue to amass more wealth, while the poor wait at the end of the pipeline for a hint of a trickle of hope; not daring to believe that actual help will come. What then is a person to do? I am glad you asked; they must take responsibility for themselves and their neighbors. How you ask, can we do that? The same way people all over the world are doing, better your living standard, first by believing that you can, and seek others who desire to better their lives, and join together to create a way to earn a sustainable income. We call it, getting in the boat.

I am not economist and have not attained a degree, but it is clear that jobs are not the only answer, because they will not come in time to salvage the lives of families that have already run out of time. If and when jobs do come, the poor must be able to master the discipline of math and science in order to obtain jobs in the twenty first century, to earn a reasonable rate of pay. If the government took the leadership, there is no reason the minimum wage could not be a minimum of twenty dollars an hour after three years of employment, thereby reducing the cost of hiring and retraining new employees.

Having served in the Army for twenty years as an administrator, I am keenly aware of the need for policies and procedures; however, when we ran across a policy or procedure that was counter-productive to the task or goal, we would change the system to solve the problem, not add to the problem through some unsustainable quick fix. A good example of change occurred when I was about to retire from the Army. In 1951 Executive Order (EO 10240 was signed by President Harry S. Truman that gave the service permission to discharge a woman if she became pregnant, or became a parent by adoption or a step-parent. Women could join the Army if they had children, but could not remain in the service if they got pregnant. When I married a female officer, who wanted a child, I partitioned the Army to make an exception because my new wife was a military intelligence officer and wore civilian clothes, to my surprise the policy was changed to allow all women to remain in service if they got pregnant, as long as they meet the guidelines of Army Regulation 600-9 on weight six months afterwards. The remainder of this book will give a blueprint wherein a man or woman can create a new way of earning long-term, sustainable income. We must go back to the old ways and develope a system that those who are attempting to escape poverty can gain access to capital, and provide an industry that can be entered by almost everyone, from anywhere, including a far-away village in deepest Africa.

We have prepared and started the process through a proven system of Micro lending. Our model is designed to assure easy entry with low interest rates and no concern for credit history. It is necessary for you to meet some of the people that we have worked with, to help you see the world from their prospective, and learn how hope stirred a glimpse of the possibility of a new beginning.

It is a story from the bottom up; the common thread for them is a renewed hope that was lost, while living in the richest country in the world, and by some who live in some of the poorest countries in the world.

This system will allow poor people to compete with the middle class and the wealthy and become members of whichever class that their dedication and hard work will carry them.

Their social status will change from being on the doll; thereby entering into the world of a card caring membership of the so called, middle or upper class, and possess all the things that signal their entry. It is this group who will empower the poor through employment or business ownership, and helping them to create a new way of viewing the world, because they will remember their own transition up the ladder and will have the desire to help others by instilling in them through our program, a renewed hope and a way to obtain their dreams. We have had great success helping extremely poor people in third world countries through micro-financing. We will utilize the micro lending model when necessary established by the Grameen Bank in Bangladesh by making "in kind"; or peer to peer or "in kind loans" loans. Unlike traditional lending institutions, our system require that we work with a of five members to establish a relationship that has little direct bearing on the repayment of their loan, but creating a community that surpass their business, we call it "A Life On The Boat."

We have a mentoring program that will train people to become micro or large farmers all over the globe and change the culture in which they have been accustomed, by giving them a sense of group self-worth and subsequently finding themselves revaluing their own worth, by training them in the art of organic farming, establishing hubs for preparing the harvest for market, and creating networks to not only sale at a swap meet, but to established markets all over the world.

We will also require our group to take courses online to learn all facets of agribusiness through one of our partners U Can Grow-Earth. Located in Johannesburg, South Africa and our in-house agronomist, who will do hands-on training to insure that we get it right the first time.

I am convinced that we are living in a time in America unlike any we have experienced in the history of this great country, with two exceptions, the Great Civil War, and the Depression of 1929. There is a war between the rich and the poor being fought on the battlefield set up for exclusion, by financial instructions all over the world. Emerging third world countries have some excuse, but America-shame on you.

As stated earlier, our government has lost the vision of our founding fathers. We are no longer a "government of the people, by the people, and for the people." We are the government where the privileged acquire great wealth, while the masses are left out of the capitalist process.

The government has divided us into two basic groups, the few who have much and the many who have almost nothing. Many in our great country and the world, are stuck in abject poverty and the government's solution to eradicate poverty (if we have one), has not, and will not work.

The so called "middle class, if there ever was one, is crumbling into the class just beneath it. Like a yellow line on the freeway, it does not belong to either side of the road, of the rich or poor, in fact, the middle class, has found themselves loaded with debt, while "running out of money before they run out of month."

This class is stuck in unfamiliar territory, one that has caused panic and blame, and instead of changing their lifestyle, they blame the government for their eventual demise. We believe that our government will change our form of government to a feudal system, of the "haves and the have not's," and eventually eliminate the so-called middle class, unless we act now.

The government cannot, or will not fix the problem, and the private sector is not interested in lending to the poor. Because of a lack of real leadership in the middle class who depend on the unions and pension funds to look out for their present and future welfare. Churches have provided the only leadership for the poor. It can make you feel good about your relationship with God, but do little to help the poor to permanently get out of physical poverty; it too has become a type of enabler, by not taking a leadership role in solving the poverty problem.

The poor has a schedule of the places and organizations that give food, vouchers, shelter, and clothing, and many are proficient at their craft of eating the crumbs from the table of the rich. I know many good men and women who do this worthy work, but my point is few help change and sustain the lives of the poor; through a system of self-empowerment, we started the proven system of lending to the poor in Kenya for micro farming; we will start by earning large amounts of money through the circular economics and the sale of AGx all over the world, in order to earn money to loan to people by January 2023. We started in Kenya and will start in Bakersfield and then to the uttermost part of the world. To get a view of the problems that poor people, black, brown and white face, we decided to paint a composite picture of a poor black man and woman. We are not painting these pictures to give the poor an excuse, but have painted each to give you an inside view, of what life is like on the other side of the tracks (Outside of the Boat). I have lived in Bakersfield for the past forty-four years with my wife Barbara Jackson-Cruise; and like many of you, God has blessed us with much in spite of the physical and spiritual conditions we sometime find ourselves; we believe our greatest gift is the gift of giving. Poverty is a serious problem that is not going away; in fact, it is going to get worse unless we do something about it. The emotions and pride of having an African American President, could not, and did not reach us on the streets and ghettos of America , where disrespect for life and violence, combined with the loss of hope is the order of the day. We, as well as some of you here in Bakersfield, have tried to help with this problem as far back as 1988 and earlier; through the efforts of men like Glenn Hierlmeier, who was the driving force in reaching out to the poor community at that time. He had a personal commitment to assist to empower poor. As the CEO of Castle and Cooke, he helped a landscaping business, with startup capital, and these new found enterprise hired seventy-five men and women who had been unemployed for three years or more, one had never had a job. These and other programs had some success, but most were not able to produce long-term benefits. I believe that Glen's efforts in the black or poor community was the chief reason that he was replaced

Since his departure, I am not aware of any minority contractors who were contracted after Hierlmier's tenure. Pull Up From Poverty is another attempt to capture our streets, and provide real hope, and in my opinion, is the only way that will allow us to help take control of our destiny, and the future of our children. We have done much with so little, and we pray that God's will continue to grace us with much, in order for us to do more to change the lives of the poor. I need not remind any of you again of how difficult; if not impossible it is for black and poor people to obtain capital from traditional sources. We tried the oft- repeated conversation that we hear at family events, "we need to start a pool and save money to start a business or to help each other. When the event ends, so does the dream. We tried to do the same thing with our family, and did not get to first base that is why Barbara and I decided to start a micro finance business in Kenya. Jesus spoke the truth when he said "a prophet is not honored in his own hometown."

You are invited to look at their history of the industry on the internet by going to Goggle and enter Grameen Bank. Their success has been phenomenal. The founder, Dr. Muhammad Yunus, won the 2006 Novel Peace Prize, along with the Bank, and was recently awarded the Medal of Peace by President Obama. Grameen America was started in Queens, New York in 2008; however, Dr. Yunus is of the opinion, that the American Woman does not have the patience to work in the Grameen System; therefore, at the time of this writing most participants are immigrants from third world countries. I strongly disagree with Dr. Yanus; however, we had to find a business model that will allow men as well as woman to quickly start a business, and still fall within the system that Grameen Bank has of making small to mid-range loans. We realize that in America the loan stakes are higher, and we are prepared to lend any amount that a business can reasonably be expected to repay in running a healthy business. This problem is a human problem; it traverses race, religion, and national origin. We must begin to look at a new, yet an old profession, The Demand Service Industry. For individuals who have not idea of what type of business they would like to own, or have no marketable skills, we would recommend a service industry; as an example, companies like Lyft or Uber, the new service that is providing transportation or services using new technology, is a perfect fit. We will lend a person who has a driver's license, and can pass a drug test, and have had no felony record for the past five years, enough money to buy a suitable car, and obtain insurance, and operating capital for three months, and of course, a new iPhone, as well as the proper training and support in order to become successful business person with a woman who we met at church and loaned money to enroll in school, to learn the business of brokering trucks for independent truckers who haul freight all over the country. Due to her critical need to earn money, we could not wait to help her through the Grameen System, my wife and I loaned her the money, and drove her to the school, when she completed the course, she started to using drugs again. Our first lesson learned, you cannot help someone who is not willing to change their lifestyle.

CHAPTER FIVE

THE REDISTRIBUTION DISCUSSION

You can visit any barber shop or beauty salon and hear conversations from the point of view of a woman as opposed to that of a man; at either place the underlying theme is the need for forty acres and a mule, a new start, a new hope, a new life.

America has so much talent and ingenuity that has gone untapped and the leadership in our country is not, and will never reach main-street ghetto, USA. There are too many reasons that can be argued as to our current condition, I am convinced and will prove that we must solve our own problems regardless of the resources of a type of forty acres and a mule.

What does a wealthy person look like, what is it that sets him or her apart from a man who is not wealthy? Wealthy people come in all shapes and forms, every color, culture and kinds. This is a how to book. It will chronicle the lives of people, who had little or nothing, with no hope and no future. A people who are unable to participate in the American Dream, to have a family, own a home and live in peace.

I have no doubt that with the help of the Lord we will make a significant impact in the lives of people who truly want to change their circumstances. Through hope, patience and hard work, and the direction by the many heroes who you will meet, whose stories will give you a renewed strength to find your peace?

In my first novel Blood Bath In Jasper County, Mississippi where I introduced the idea of micro financing that we started in Kenya on May 11, 2008; after determining that the system created by Dr. Mohammad Yanus, and the Grameen Bank we decided to bring the concept to America. Before my first novel was off the press, I decided that I would write a second novel that would document people who came from a place where there is no hope, and help them to become productive and hopefully introduce them to the only power that is true power, the Lord Jesus Christ.

I have interviewed hundreds of people who were willing to share their personal stories in their attempt to answer the question, "how did I get to this point in my life?"

There are untold thousands of people who have dreams of a better life, but most of them have no direction. This book is a lab that has allowed you to look at each person as they tell their personal story. How they were born or moved into poverty and through the grace of God got involved in this great God-Breathed work.

They will tell you about the things that they have accomplished, or hope to accomplish, because of their involvement in this project, and about their hope and dreams for the future. Before my friends and associates "jump down my throat," let us clear up this idea of wealth. For me, it is having enough for myself and my family and purposefully plan to help others to do the same thing. We all know that money has its limits, and there are many old sayings, explaining what money can't buy. All of us know and may have experienced it ourselves, that money does not in itself bring inner peace. Inner peace for me in knowing from within what I was told by my Barber, Robert Key's father, who often said, "Nothing and no one can beat me on my best day." The problem that most of our youth face is the lack of a "best days." I continue to see young men substituting the things that should be nourished in the home is hopelessly sought after in neighborhood gangs. The negative model carries with it a mentality of what I term "zero emotions," a mentality that says my life is leading to nowhere, therefore life has no value. I cannot tell anyone how I feel, that I do not have a feeling of worth; a feeling that I have no one to share my fears, or my dreams and in most cases, no means to obtain money to get started. Those who are trapped in this capitalistic society see no way out. I am not loved and I don't love, because I don't know how to love. I am sure that deep down inside I am headed to prison or to the grave. I have no respect for myself nor for my women; I take whatever I can get by any means available to me. Only a few people know that I can't read and can barely write my name. I could not recognize my name if it was being towed by an airplane across the sky. I am convinced that my only out is to take any and everything that I can. The people who were fortunate enough to bypass most of the trials and tribulations of being poor, have not only abandoned the neighborhood where they were brought up and moved two or three zip codes away, do not have system to reach back to help the next generation to redistribute a small portion of their increase. It is our hope to find such men and women

We must erase the house slave mentality viruses' those of the field hand that the field hand, that the reason we made it, is we worked harder than those without. This attitude is one of the major reasons that we have lost the community spirit and the family spirit as witnessed in Armstrong Colony, Texas. We must begin not only to share our wealth, but our knowledge and our wisdom to our people and any person who has the desire to change their lives.

The wall that has divided white people from black people, and the rich from the poor, must be torn down just as surely that the wall was destroyed in Berlin. No man in his right mind can lay claim to his good or his greatness, less he be labeled a fool.

CHAPTER SIX

THE ANSWER

We have established a Non-Profit who will empower the poor through "Peer to Peer lending. In most cases we may help those who have no idea of what they would do if capital was available. This system is not new, it started through the effort recently famous economist, and founder of the Grameen Bank in Bangladesh in October 1983. He and the bank received the Nobel Prize Dr. Yanus also received the Presidential Medal of Freedom and the Congressional Medal from the United States Congress. Dr. Yanus started with forty-seven women in 1976, and has built a financial empire all over the world, in less than forty years

At first, he did not think that his system would be successful in America, but changed his mind, when he started Grameen New York, where he started lending money to first generation immigrants, manly from the Dominican Republic. Grameen is now called Grameen America, and have partnered with Citi Bank to make loans using the Grameen System. Citi Bank is to be applauded for the vision in this exciting new monetary delivery system. Our system will differ in the method used to repay the loans. Instead of an extended repayment period, we will only seek repayment when we help the borrower make money, otherwise the debt will be forgiven debt write-off or self-insurance, including natural disasters. The insurance will be paid by the lender.

CHAPTER SEVEN

WHAT IS WRONG WITH US

It is not clear why poor people have not had a champion to rise up and help them escape the ravages of poverty. Men have arisen to national and international prominence, men who emerged from the culture of poverty, Fredrick Douglas, Dr. Martin Luther King, Jr quickly come to mind.

They offered hope without financial empowerment. They fought and gains equal rights, but they did not have a business model to move the masses into the mainstream of American Life as promised by the Constitution and the famous speech by President Lincoln at Gettysburg Pennsylvania.

As we looked and listened to the last presidential debates of 2012, neither candidate, Democrat or Republican,, made any promises directly to the poor of this great country, because the only remedy that they had, was a continuance of the same old promises, to improve the middle class with the hope of a "trickle down" the effect from their new found prosperity, but nothing has changed, the poor continue to be enabled, by the government with no attempt to empower them.

The few times that they ventured to use the word poor, was in the context of helping the middle class by creating jobs which will increase the tax base that will provide jobs for the poor, when in fact they continue to provide welfare to the poor. Self-help is the only way that will change the lives of the poor.

Our work in Kenya has taught us how to empower the poor through the intervention of Non-governmental Organizations or (NGOs). NGOs have been in existence in America in most major cities in this country before the turn of the century; however, most of them were organized to empower groups who had a common bond such as religion, race or national origin the one exception is poor black people.

We cannot mention the new civil war without mentioning the new slavery. It is so unrecognizable that it is almost impossible to see, although it is right in front of our faces.

I remember with great pleasure the day that I learned about the men who lived in Armstrong Colony, Texas a few years after the Civil War. They resolved to not only better themselves, but to help their neighbors improve their lot in life. I recall the same feelings in nineteen seventy-four, the year that I retired from the Army.

I was told about a group of thirteen men who had filtered through the screen of poverty and became successful business men. Nobody knew who they were except those who received their help.

They were a mixture of businessmen, clergy and unsung heroes who had acquired a comfortable lifestyle. Only two of them were wealthy, but together they help change the lives of an untold number of people who were not satisfied with their station in life, and wanted more for themselves and their families.

I was introduced to them by a young man who was reputed to be the best black golfer in Atlanta; (I have long-sensed forgotten his name), he worked at Norell Security at night and hustled on the local golf courses during the day.

I played a round of golf with him, because I wanted to improve my game. Although he was well dressed, his teeth were in a deplorable state. After our round, I asked about his teeth, and he said he could not afford to get them fixed.

The Apostle Peter in me, made a spontaneous decision and decided right then, and there, that I wanted to open a dental clinic in the middle of the Atlanta ghetto, that would be staffed by dentists from Meharry School of Dentistry located in Nashville, Tennessee. I had never heard of this great institution until I hired one of its staff dentists. A recent graduate who had just passed the dental state board, on the condition that we would build a clinic.

The college was named for a young Scottish immigrant salt trader named Samuel Meharry, who was traveling through the rough terrain of Tennessee when his wagon suddenly slipped off the road and fell into a swamp. Meharry was helped by a family of freedmen, whose names are unknown.

This family of freed slaves gave Meharry food and shelter in the night. The next morning they helped him to recover his wagon. Meharry is reported to have told the former slave family, "I have no money, but when I can, I shall do something for your race."

In 1875, Samuel Meharry, together with four of his brothers, donated a total of $15,000 to assist with the establishment of a medical department at Central Tennessee College with a contribution of the Freedman's Aid Society of the Methodist Episcopal Church North the school was opened.

George W. Hubbard and John Braden, a Methodist cleric, were able to open the Medical Department of Central Tennessee College in 1876. The first class had one graduate. The second class, which had its commencement in 1878, had three graduates. In 1886, the Dental Department was founded, followed by a Pharmacy Department that was founded in 1889.

Among the second class of graduates was Lorenzo Dow Key, the son of Hillary- Wattsworth-Key. Key, together with Braden, was one of the founding members of the Tennessee Conference of the Methodist Episcopal Church, North. The church had split into Methodist Episcopal Church North and Methodist Episcopal Church South on the issue of slavery and was not reunited until 1939.

In 1900, Central Tennessee College changed its name to Walden University in honor of John Morgan Walden, a bishop of the Methodist Church who had ministered to freedmen. In 1915, the medical department faculty of Walden University received a separate charter as Meharry Medical College.

It included the departments of pharmacy and dentistry. The Medical College remained in its original buildings, and Walden University moved to another campus in Nashville. Hubbard served as Meharry Medical College's first president until his death in 1921.

Meharry is the second largest educator of African-American medical doctors and dentists in the United States. It is also the largest producer of African Americans with Masters in Public Health and Ph.D.'s in biomedical science.

We purchased a large, rundown brick building that was commonplace in Southwest Atlanta in 1978. I had enough money to renovate the building, but needed two hundred thousand dollars for used equipment. After closing on the property, one of the members of the group, who was a very successful general contractor, volunteered to renovate the building at cost. The group was instrumental in our obtaining a letter of credit with the only black bank in Atlanta, and we were on our way.

About half way through the project, the dentist changed his mind and went into private practice in Memphis, Tennessee I had worked so hard to make this dream a reality, I was so despondent; I sold the building and moved to Bakersfield, California. You might wonder why we are sharing this story, it is to show that people have tried to empower others but on a small scale, some are successful and others, as in my case were not.

I believe that most have failed because they did not include God in their plan, for fear that some might say this is not what the church is here for. I have learned that the way the early church had favor with all of the people, was their sensitivity to the needs of the people and their desire to help satisfy their needs.

We must reach out, and not be afraid to go in the name of the Lord. Jesus fed people, as he was teaching them about the Kingdom. After our work started to empower people in Kenya, many came wanting to be baptized into Christ, because they thought it would get them a loan faster. We simply told them that being a Christian was not a requirement to obtaining a loan. We finally had to place a sign on our building in Swahili and Luo to make sure that everybody would understand.

Yet many still come with the idea of using obedience to the gospel as a type of collateral in exchange for money or food. We continue to reject their request.

Currently churches in Kenya are going to be regulated because of fraud perpetrated on uneducated poor people, and claims of being able to heal people, while they pocket large amounts of money.

We realize the possible pit-falls that we could fall into, despite our good intentions in the beginning. Dr.Yunus first thought that micro lending would not work in America, but has since changed his mind and is helping mostly women in cities like New York, Detroit, Los Angeles, to name a few.

We are prepared to unleash the new emancipation, one of capital acquisition by people who have never recovered from the abyss of slavery and discrimination and defeat the master plan of the rich, to keep poor people poor.

We have seen firsthand what a person can do to better their life if given an equal chance to compete in the world of finance. Many in this group or slaves to their FICO Score (myself included), will be freed and granted loans based on their character, and a business plan that make good business sense.

We place our applicants into a group of five people, who are also required to attend a thirty-day training class, pass a drug test, and complete the course. Applicants, who have drug issues, will be sent to a treatment program for up to a year. The cost will be prepaid by the corporation, and added to their loan.

When we have a group of five identified, the group will decide who will obtain the first two loans, after three weeks of successful weekly repayment, the same group decides who will receive the next two loans, and after three additional successful payments by the second group, the last applicant is given a loan.

When the group is established, we do not do a credit check, and the applicant is not required to sign a contract for a loan less than two hundred and fifty thousand dollars.

Applicants who do not have a checking and saving accounts will be required to open a bank account. We may also require each applicant to establish a burial fund and a hospital fund.

Each group will be assigned a counselor who will visit them or contact the group via internet, each week to ensure that things are going according to their plan, taking into consideration that circumstances do occur in the best business model, when there is a problem, the counselor will make a conference call with the group, and try to solve whatever issues that is causing a problem for the group. Our creed is, if one is ill, all are sick; if one is successful, all are successful.

We establish very early in the process, that we are responsible to help each other to succeed. There is no better example of this, than the story of the "Sugar Cane Ladies" in Kenya. They pull for each other and together represent the model that we will attempt to instill in all of our groups.

As previously stated, the example of Armstrong Colony, Texas how people found value in a common bond. As I read their story, it spurred me to continue our quest to help the poor, and to never give up this larger- than-life dream.

In spite of the obstacles these people with almost nothing, over a period of time, with the help and support of each other, changed the lives of their families and their decedents.

The following story is included by permission of Carolyn Heinholsm

CHAPTER EIGHT

ARMSTRONG COLONY TEXAS

I recently learned about a group of ex-slaves who lived in a place called Armstrong Colony, Texas. They agreed to purchase land from a common treasury and divide the land among themselves. Many descendants from that group continue to prosper to this day. They held their one hundred and thirty fourth gala in twenty twelve. Here is an article that I believe will increase your faith in our project. We salute them for their example of a village working together.

Unlike the ex-slaves in Armstrong Colony, most of us are blinded by race, religion, and what I call social retardation. We cannot come to a common agreement that if change is to come, we must make it happen, instead of binding together, it is point our past attempts at self-help. Look at what happened to a group of people who had little, but accomplished a great deal.

ARMSTRONG COLONY — A FREEDMEN'S SETTLEMENT
A Footprints of Fayette article by **Carolyn Heinsohn**

Other than the written history of a community church, the stories about Armstrong Colony seem to be oral family traditions, passed down from one generation to another. With time, some facts are forgotten, and stories change. Therefore, the author has made an effort to compile the known documented facts into a written history. Hopefully, the community's rich oral history will continue to be told by the descendants of the founders of this freedmen's settlement.

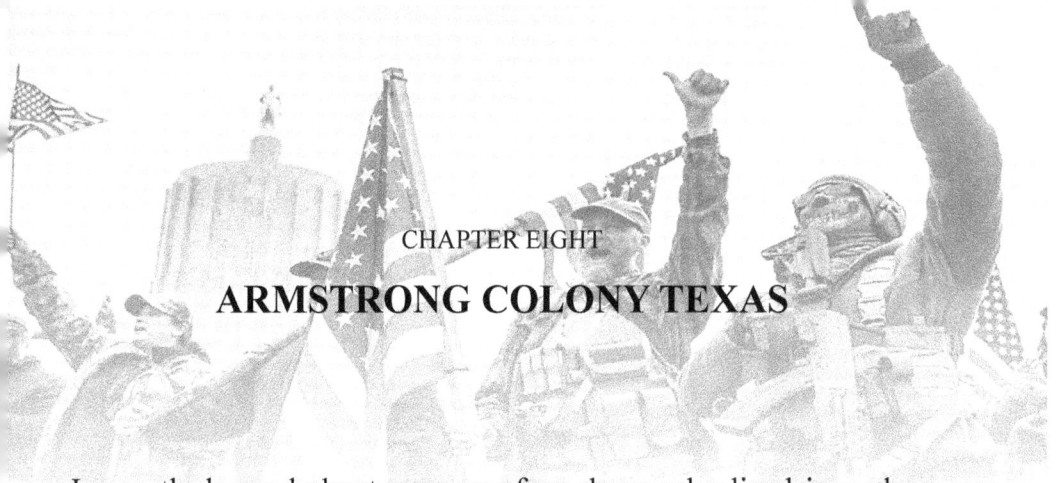

Located eight miles west of Flatonia in southwestern Fayette County near the point where Gonzales, Lavaca and Fayette Counties meet, the Armstrong Colony is one of two freedmen's settlements in the county. The other community is Cozy Corner, which is located at the intersection of FM 155 and Co. Rd. 3233, approximately five miles south of La Grange.

Freedmen's settlements, which primarily were formed in the eastern half of Texas in the years after Emancipation, were informal, independent rural communities of freed African-American landowners and land squatters, who were predominantly farmers and stockmen.

These settlements, which were sometimes called "freedom colonies" by the African-American settlers, were somewhat of an anomaly in Texas after the Civil War where white elites rapidly resumed economic, political and social control, and sharecropping became prevalent in the agricultural system that previously had been based on slave labor.

The formation of these independent black communities was motivated by the freedmen's desires for land, autonomy and isolation from the whites. Even though the 1865 rumor that the federal government would provide all ex-slaves with "40 acres and a mule" proved to be false, a minority of the freedmen set out to achieve that dream, and some of them succeeded in establishing themselves on pockets of wilderness, cheap land, or neglected land previously little utilized for cotton production. The majority of the freedmen, however, took employment with white landowners as day laborers, sharecroppers or share tenants.

Some of the slaves were actually freed prior to Emancipation for a variety of reasons. Occasionally, a white plantation owner would free his mulatto progeny and their slave mothers. Whether freed or not, certain favored slaves were given the privilege to work in the plantation house and were sometimes allowed to learn to read and write.

Perhaps this exposure to a different world other than fieldwork and heavy labor, plus the opportunity to receive a rudimentary education, planted the seed that then germinated after Emancipation, providing the impetus for some of the freedmen to venture away from their plantation locations.

They sought a new life that they hoped would offer far greater opportunities for their families than what was available to them at that time. Plus, they understood that education was a tool to effectively function in a literate society, so oftentimes they supported the early establishment of schools in their new communities.

The founders of the Armstrong Colony were among that minority group, who took the risk to re-locate and had the fortitude to seek a new life in a community that they themselves created. Although it was un-platted, unincorporated and never had its own post office, the Armstrong Colony was unified by a church, schools and several scattered businesses.

One of the first to arrive in the area was the family of Jacob and Eliza Armstrong with their four children. The 1870 census lists them as first living in Precinct 3 in Lavaca County. Enumerated were Jacob, a farmer, age 52, born circa 1818; Eliza J., age 45, born circa 1825; Mitchel, age 25; Rachel, age 20; Frank, age 17; and Sarah, age 15. More than likely Jacob was a sharecropper.

According to family tradition related by a descendant, Felton Armstrong, the Jacob Armstrong family came to Texas in 1865 from Lafayette, Louisiana. However, the 1870 census records indicate that Jacob was born in Mississippi. His wife, Eliza, and children were also born in Mississippi, although records indicate that Eliza's parents were born in Alabama. Perhaps the entire family was sold to a Louisiana plantation owner, so they were forced to move to Lafayette sometime before their emancipation and subsequent move to Texas.

One of Jacob's neighbors in Lavaca County in 1870 was Sam Bilton, born circa 1842 in Tennessee, and wife, Charlotte, born circa 1848 in Missouri, along with their five children. Another child was born later in 1870 after the census was taken. Peter Grant, age 28 from Louisiana; his 20-year old wife, Ann, who was born in Mississippi, and their three young children were living nearby, so probably were working on the same land. They would later become neighbors again in Armstrong Colony.

In December, 1875, Jacob Armstrong purchased 162 acres of land on the head waters of Peach Creek in Fayette County, approximately 25 miles southwest of La Grange, from G.C. McGregor and E.H. Fortran for $755.00. He paid $5.00 down with five promissory notes of $150.00 each.

In the 1880 census, Jacob, age 63, was listed as living in Precinct 6 of Fayette County in the area that is now known as Armstrong Colony, along with his second wife, Louise, age 62; daughter, Rachel, age 29; widowed daughter, Selena/Sarah Garrett, age 26, along with her six children, and three grandchildren.

Jacob's sons, Mitchel and Frank, and their families were also living on his property. Mitchel (1843-1904) married Fanny Bilton (1854-1939), daughter of Sam Bilton, possibly before moving to Fayette County. In 1889, Jacob sold 82 acres of his farm to his son, Mitchel, for $100 and a promise that he would pay one-half of the unpaid balance on the notes for his original 162 acres, probably because Jacob was unable to pay for the notes on time. He also sold 14 acres to his grandson, Ellard, for $50 and a promise to pay one-fourth of the unpaid balance on his notes. Ellard was able to purchase another 16 acres that were located adjacent to his grandfather's property from McGregor and Fortran for a total of 30 acres.

Actually, the first freedmen family to move to the area that became Armstrong Colony was Harry Simms (1848–1911), born in Texas, the son of Brutes and Ferberry Simms, and his mulatto wife, Ellen Pettit, (1845-1927), daughter of Harvey and Adeline Pettit, and their children.. The parents of Ellen Simms were either from Arkansas or Tennessee, but were living in Gonzales County when they sold 100 acres of land on Peach Creek to their daughter and son-in-law, who also were living in Precinct 3 of Gonzales County, for $160 in July, 1874.

The 1900 census indicates that Harry and Ellen had been married for 34 years and had nine living children. Although Harry's tombstone indicates that his birth year was 1839, several documents indicate that he was actually born circa 1848.

The Frank Derry family moved into the community after the Armstrong's. In March, 1877, Frank Derry and his wife, Mariah, purchased 102 acres approximately 30 miles west of La Grange from N.W. Brown for $500. In the 1880 census, Frank Derry, born circa 1827 in Alabama, was shown to be living in Fayette County with his mulatto wife, Maria, born circa 1832 in North Carolina, and their nine children, a nephew and a niece. One of their daughters, Clemmie, was married to Emmette Simms, the son of aforementioned Harry and Ellen Simms.

Frank and Mariah later purchased an additional 100 acres on the waters of Peach Creek. They eventually sold 30 acres from each of their tracts of land to their two sons, Alex and Charley, plus another 34 acres to A.B. Kerr of Muldoon. By 1899, Marie had died, and Frank, age 71, married Melindy, age 55. In 1900, he was living in Armstrong Colony with a mix of children, grandchildren and a step-grandson. By 1910, Melindy must have died, because she was not enumerated in the census, and Frank was living with his daughter, Clemmie, her husband and their eight children.

The Sam Bilton family is also documented as one of the early families of the community. Sam purchased 150 acres on Peach Creek in the Menefee League from John Cline for $1200 in November, 1889. He had three unassigned promissory notes for $400 each; however, he was unable to pay the notes, so he was forced to sell his land and have the notes assigned to T.M. Connon of Flatonia. However, Bilton's three sons, Sam, Jr., A.B. and William, agreed to collaboratively pay the notes in order to keep the family land.

Others continued to find their way to the growing community, some of whom were the Browns, Burlesons, Grants, Greens, Henrys, Hunts, Jones, McKinnons, Nunns, Perpeners, Sanders, Warrens, Winkfields and Usserys.

The Bureau of Refugees, Freedmen and Abandoned Lands, commonly known as the Freedmen's Bureau, that was established by Congress in 1865, provided relief to the thousands of refugees, black and white, who had been left homeless by the Civil War. Many blacks turned to the agency for protection, advice or help in finding lost relatives.

Although the Bureau was dissolved in July, 1870, it was most successful in Texas with its educational efforts. It helped establish 150 schools in the state with an enrollment of over 9,000 students. Perhaps, the Bureau influenced Jacob Armstrong and other nearby freedmen to establish a school for their children on Armstrong's land soon after his purchase.

The "school" was actually a brush arbor that had seats hewn from logs. Inclement weather would have been a definite factor influencing school attendance, but at least there was an effort to educate the children in the community, which was named after Jacob Armstrong, since he provided the land for the school and eventually the church.

Jacob Armstrong's son, Frank, who married Clara Washington, was one of the first deacons of Armstrong Colony's newly-founded Mt. Olive Church, along with Sam Bilton. The church, which was founded under the direction of Professor and Reverend O.E. Perpener, the first teacher and pastor, was organized in 1876 in the brush arbor that was serving as the "schoolhouse".

The history of the church states that there were eight persons in the first church organization – six members of the Armstrong family and Rev. Perpener and his wife. As others moved into the area, they soon were sending their children to the school and attending the open-air church, which became the social center of the community.

At first the church members met for prayer meetings on Wednesday nights, being called to worship by Jacob, who would blow a cow horn when it was time to meet. Light was provided by bottles filled with kerosene that burned with wicks of flannel rags. The church, which became known as the Mt. Olive Missionary Baptist Church, was eventually moved to a log cabin where services were held, and school was taught. An active Mission Society was later founded by the women of the congregation.

In 1914, Rev. F.D. Davis, a young dynamic minister, accepted the position of pastor of Mt Olive. Under his direction, the Baptist Training Union and a youth group were organized. He also launched a building program to create a new church building, which was completed in 1918 on an acre of land donated by Fannie Armstrong and Charlotte Bilton.

That church, which had an interesting architectural design, was eventually in need of restoration, but instead it was razed and replaced by the present brick sanctuary in 1994. A fellowship hall stands nearby, and the Mt. Olive Museum and Cultural Center filled with historical documents, photographs and memorabilia of the community is located in the old "teacherage", a structure that housed black teachers during segregation.

At one time, there not only was a primary school in the community, but also a high school known as the Albrecht School, both of which prepared many young people for college educations and careers in all walks of life across the United States. By 1992, there were 27 descendants of the first families who had obtained their college education at Prairie View College. The total number of graduates from other collegiate institutions is not documented, but undoubtedly, these families valued the importance of an education for their children.

Although the church and school were the spiritual, educational and social centers of the community, the Armstrong General Store, Cue Bilton General Store, Marvin Brown Store and Needham Store provided the necessities for the local people during the era when there was a larger population in the area, and transportation to Waelder or Flatonia was difficult. There were two gins operated by the Winkfield and Derry families when cotton production was significant enough to necessitate their existence.

The Derrys also had a broom factory. The only remaining evidence of the once-thriving, small community is the church-museum complex on Armstrong-Derry Road, a well-kept cemetery located a short distance away, and the residences of a few remaining families, some of whom are descendants of the original families.

In the late 1940s and early 1950s, oil was discovered in the area, so some of the families were fortunate enough to benefit from the short-lived oil production before the wells went dry. For those families with land and retained mineral rights, the newest oil boom related to drilling in the Eagleford Shale will provide some much-appreciated future income.

The majority of the descendants of those strong, pioneering freedmen, who pursued their dreams and persevered in their labors to carve out a livelihood in a community that they created, have spread out like the branches of a mighty oak, but their roots are still in the Armstrong Colony. Many return annually every August for the community homecoming event to reunite with their families and reconnect to their special heritage.

Sources: "Armstrong Colony's Mt. Olive Baptist Church 116th Anniversary and Homecoming" booklet; 1992 Census records for 1870, 1880, 1900 and 1910 from Ancestry.com Deed records; Fayette County Clerk

Personal interviews with Felton Armstrong and Volna Derry Thad Sutton, "Freedmen's Settlements". Handbook of Texas Online; published by the Texas State Historical Association

CHAPTER NINE

A COMPOSITE OF A POOR BLACK WOMAN IN AMERICA

This sketch of a young black woman in America is not designed to belittle or berate black women. It has been drawn in the same manner a police artist compose a picture based on an eye witness account of what one saw or lived. I have talked to over a hundred women who told their story and later saw the composite, more than ninety percent and of them agreed that it was, in many ways, their picture. I am sure that you have a family member or a friend or co-worker who will fit this description-some of whom may be Caucasian or some other ethnic group. For the sake of clarity, we will paint two pictures, the first is a woman between the ages of sixteen and thirty-five who did not graduate from high school. There are countless variables that could change the picture but we have chosen just two.

Over eighty percent of this group came from a broken home or a single parent home. This group tended to have their first child between the ages of fourteen to seventeen years old. Approximately fifteen percent of them completed high school after their first child was born, and enrolled in college or a technical school; over sixty percent of those who did not complete high school and participate in academic or vocational education, had a second child before they were twenty years old. Out this group an astonishing seventy percent had their second child by a different "baby's daddy," and twenty percent of this group had a third child by a third man.

Her life is one of total dependency on the welfare system. She does not arrive at this point overnight because she still has a slight glimmer of hope that she will escape the ravages of poverty. She is caught in a web of trying to live with her children and the different number of daddy's that are directly or indirectly involved in her life until one day she succumbs, and finally give up hope.

The women who complete high school seek some form of employment. They usually find subsidized housing and obtain a minimum wage job. The men in her life have little respect for her and usually have been to prison, or, they are in prison, or on parole. When the chosen one is released from prison he finds his baby's mother working and has been able to buy a car.

His first day out of jail is a happy reunion and he ask but mostly inform his woman that he need the car to go and "kick it" with his friends. She reluctantly gives him the car after he drops her off at work with the promise to pick her up at ten that night. She has to catch a ride with a co-worker and he returns at three in the morning.

She is furious because she recognizes the same pattern from the last time he was released from jail; she tells him that he cannot use the car on the days she has to work. After a heated argument he hurls the keys at her and storms out of the house, he then hurls a rock through the windshield and he completes the job by "keying" her car as he storms down the walkway. When to police arrive he is returned to jail for parole violation, and oftentimes this pattern is repeated.

After a series of similar disappoints with other men she eventually loses her job and has no transportation and eventually lose all hope of changing her life. Now every facet of her life is subject to and dependent on the government to live a life without hope.

The woman who graduates from high school but has similar experiences with having children and men differ in that it appears to take longer to reach the stage of hopelessness and despair. This group tend to be able to work in jobs that pay a little more but in many cases the cost of transportation and clothes does not allow them to live any better than when they were on welfare.

They too return to the system that enables, but does not empower them. When drugs are part of the problem, the situation worsens in that they either lose their children to the state or they are placed with a relative. Most of these women are motivated by the misguided idea that they can continue to live the same lifestyle and somehow get their children back.

In fairness to those who do not fit this description, there are countless thousands who filter through the screen of poverty although they did not live in a healthy environment; somehow they escape this great dilemma. When I talk with some of these women I ask all of them the same question, if there was a way that they could start their own business they all say yes, but when I ask them to call and make an appointment most of them never call. Maybe this book will help them to gain a flicker of hope that their life can change.

CHAPTER TEN

COMPOSIT PICTURE OF A POOR BLACK MAN

The plight of a poor black man must be painted with a different brush. In part because this composite is based on observation of over one thousand men who worked for me from1990 to 2000, We will look at two groups as we again acknowledge that there are many who escape poverty by filtering through the maze of issues that face most black men in the environment in which they grew up in. This portrait is not intended to belittle or berate black men, as my father use to say "if the shoe fits, wear it.

Group one and two have several things in common, they were born into a society where the playing field was not level because the terrible conditions that they faced while they were in slavery. After President Lincoln set us free, it was clear that we were on the bottom rung looking up. We endured the southern gentile's attempt to re-enslave us mentally and kept us in a place of surviving by bending to the rules, or making new rules such as the "Black Code". In order to better understand our plight, it is necessary to go back to the days when black men were considered as chattel.

Black men who were enslaved dreamed of the day that they would be free. They had no reason to dream the impossible; yet they looked for the eventful day. After they were set free they married and raised large families and many of them owned land. After reconstruction the Black Code was passed that severely hindered the ability for black men to find jobs. The Klu Klux Klan only added to the burden of being a black man in America's South.

They were taught at an early age that they had to be twice as good as a white person in order to attain the same status. Many were shut out of society's main stream and were not allowed to receive the benefits of living outside of the poverty line. These and other barriers hindered the economic and social growth of a people who were looking for a better life. Thousands migrated from the south to find new opportunities in the north. They brought a healthy outlook to their families. Many remained poor but stressed education to their children. Just prior to World War Two most black families included a father and mother. After the war jobs were available for anybody who wanted to work. When the system of welfare was instituted during President Roosevelt's last term, ushered in a system that was more damaging than physical slavery.

In Illinois and other states, a woman who applied for welfare had to state that her husband was not living in the home. I personally recall that hurtful day that we were told that our father had to move out of our home. The social workers acted as policeman. They would literally stake out our house to determine if our father was living with us.

Although my mother was a strong no nonsense woman she could not give her ten boys the things that boys can only get from their father. It was the beginning of the end for poor black families.

Mothers were forced to try to raise their boys without the influence of their husbands, and men began to feel the pain of a new slave master, a feeling of not being the man of the house, just as his ancestors felt during the physical enslavement that they were forced to endure. The only person who they felt that they had power over was the black women many of them they took out their frustration on their wives.

We have banded together like the ex-slaves in Armstrong Colony, Texas, and are blessed to assist in removing many from a life of poverty, to a life of hope that the future will yield the ideals that our founding fathers had in mind, that all men are created equal.

The following five chapters are presented to draw a contrast between success and failure. They are presented as a result of personal interviews conducted in 2012.

CHAPTER ELEVEN

ROBERTA NICHOLS-ALLEN, RN
GRIT AND DETERMINATION FROM
INTERVIEW 2009

Roberta Allen was born in Seminole, Oklahoma, (Seminole County, at an Indian Church). Her parents were John and Elnora Nichols. She is from a family of eleven (11) children; five girls and six boys. Her father did not mind in the least to do hard work. He was a school teacher, bus driver, Postmaster, carpenter and Sheriff in Lima, Oklahoma. Her parents lived to see all of their children receive an education, and able to make an independent living. Sister Allen graduated from Douglas High School, in Wewoka, Oklahoma in 1937. She enrolled and attended Langston University, in Langston, Oklahoma; however, e the university did not have a nursing program, and she left after one semester, and returned home and obtained work in the Post Office, until she got her "two issues." (pay checks). She went to Kansas City, Kansas, but due to illness, she returned home for six months. She was still determined to become a registered nurse, she left Oklahoma again, and attended Emily Estes Snede-Care Nurse Training School in Tuscaloosa, Alabama, it was a Presbyterian School that offered four years of training. Upon completion she, took and passed, the State Board Examination, and became a Registered Nurse.

Her first job was with TCI General Hospital, in Birmingham, Alabama where she remained for six months. Her first month pay was a grand sum of $98.00, some of which, she deposited into the bank. Her second job was in a maternity hospital in North Birmingham, Alabama, where she was employed for approximately four months.

She came to Bakersfield in 1946. Her parents had moved here while she was in school in Alabama. She did not like Bakersfield, and "cried for a week." She became the FIRST BLACK REGISTERED NURSE, at that time it was called, Kern General Hospital. She said that when she applied for a job, she was informed the telephone operator at the information desk, that they did not "hire Black Registered Nurses."

She later contacted Mrs. Alma Estes, The Director of Nurses, and was hired on the spot. Sister Allen said that "even though I went through some trying occasions, the nurses and doctors were overly protective of me."

I broke the barrier; it paid off." Several months later, three Black Registered Nurses were hired, and the rest is history. She worked at Kern Medical Center for 23 1/2 years, after which she did private duty nursing for 26 years.

She was instrumental in helping Mr. Del Rucker, the Mortician, who was the first organizer-owner of Rucker's Mortuary, obtain his first client. (Although she did ask Mr. Rucker to pick up a body, I think she was making a self-depreciating remark about losing a patient).

After retiring in 1973, she began taking blood pressures for senior citizens, on California Avenue, and continued to provide the valuable service at the Senior Center at 430 4th Street until a few months before she died.

She met and married Efon Allen in 1974 and remained married until his death in 1996. She has resided inthe same home on Chester Place for 44 years.

Mrs. Allen was a founding member of the National Council of Negro Women (NCNW)-Bakersfield, since 1956.Mrs. Marie Fambrough was the organizer and first President. They met in the homes of its members.

Mrs. Allen became President in 1962, during her presidency the National Convention was held here in63. The convention was well attended and Mrs. Ferrall Bobo, of Los Angeles, California, was the District Supervisor.

The convention was well attended by all the local members, as well as member from Los Angeles, Fresno, Oakland and San Francisco. Sister Allen was the Treasurer for two years and the Chaplin until she died.

Mrs. Allen was baptized into Christ in Ensly, Alabama, in 1945, under the leadership of Brother F. Thompson. When she came to Bakersfield in 1946, the black Christians met in the Mexican Hall on 19th Street until they moved to the Baker Street location. In the spring of the year, Brother R.N. Hogan, Brother Marshal Kible.

Brother Russell Moore would come and run a tent meeting for a week and sometime for two weeks. She said the she knew Brother Moore better than she did the other brothers, because Brother Moore became the local Minister and helped to build the church membership to a total of one hundred and twenty members.

CHAPTER TWELVE

BARBARA JACKSON-CRUISE, RN
GRIT AND DETERMINATION FROM
INTERVIEW 2009

My story about self is not much different than that of most black girls who were born here in Bakersfield, California; many families were large in number, possibly because of the tradition of having large families or the need to earn additional money in the farm labor industry, a job that was readily available to black people at that time. My father Henry Jackson, Jr., was from a family of eighteen and was one of four sets of twins.

He married my mother Vassie Lee Gibson-Jackson in 1939 in Blyth, California. My mother had one son, James Bell and my father had four children, three boys and one girl, Harold, Clifford, Dillard, and Osa Lee; together they had eight more children, Marie, Lawrence, myself, Edward, Daaiah, Margie, Vernell and Andre. All of them have passed except Marie, myself, and Andre. My mother who celebrated her one hundred and first birthday in July, 2021 is fond of saying that they came to Bakersfield in late 1939 with five children and five dollars.

We worked in the fields picking cotton, chopping cotton and harvesting every fruit and vegetable you can name as well as potatoes in Idaho. It was always hard to return to school late and have to take special classes to catch up with our classmates. Our early life revolved around school and field work.

My older brothers were great athletes while attending Bakersfield High School, and my brother Dillard won the All-Army Heavyweight Championship in 1956 and later had a brief professional career.

I had my first child Randy Dunn when I was eighteen years old which caused me to drop out of Bakersfield High School, mostly because of the way it was in those days. I met and married Tommie Buchanan when Randy was a small boy, and had two more children, Eric, and a daughter Marla. Eric was shot by a Bakersfield Policeman under some questionable circumstances on his twenty second birthday.

I went back to adult school night and graduated from high school, while working full time sewing bags at what was known as the bag factory. It was funny how I got that job, I went to apply for a job, and the manager thought I was an employee, and told me to go to work.

At the end of the day I asked about my time card and the man who told me to go to work asked me who hired me, I told him that he is the one who told me to go to work, he smiled and said you are hired, because I had caught on, and kept up with others who had been there a long time.

Life was difficult for me because my husband did not have a steady job, and eventually went to prison. I ended up on welfare, but was determined from day one that it was not going to be forever.

My brother Lawrence was attending Bakersfield College, and suggested that I enroll at Bakersfield College and complete my prerequisites and go into nursing because my sister Margie, who was murdered while standing in my parent's driveway, was a Licensed Vocational Nurse (LVN). Upon completion of my prerequisites, I applied for entry into the LVN Program.

When I informed my social worker, and she told me about a new program called WIN, it was a new program that paid my rent, my utilities, baby sitting and would have paid my car note had I owned a car at the time of entry.

I was accepted into the License Vocational Nursing Program. Although it was difficult, I completed the course and was licensed as an LVN by the state of California.

After working a Mercy Hospital for several years in their intensive care unit, after I realized that I did almost the same thing that the Registered Nurses did in the Unit, and decided to return to school and complete my degree as a Registered Nurse.

During my last semester I met my husband Matthew Cruise, who is also my brother in Christ, and my biggest fan and friend. In a whirlwind courtship that is well chronicled in his book Blood Bath In

Jasper County, Mississippi, we married ninety days after we met on May thirty first nineteen seventy nine.

I retired as a Registered Nurse when I turned sixty five after working over thirty five years in various hospitals. As I look back and see how far I have come, physically and spiritually, I am positive that we will reach our goal to help people change their lives.

Our marriage is not perfect but we labor each day to strive for perfection. Our life would be different yet not as rewarding, if Matthew was not a dreamer, who sometimes have dreamed the impossible, because he has always tried to help people some of whom did not want to be helped. Along the way, we have owned five different businesses.

In 1990 we had over seven thousand direct sales associate in our company. But I must say, the experiences that we shared, has brought us to the now. A time when most people retire, but Matthew quietly remind me, that Moses was eighty when he was called.

I have watched my husband learn hard lessons, many of which hurt us financially and caused us much stress in our marriage and some distrust in his judgment.

He is so eager to want the best for others, some of whom who do not want the best for themselves. He contacted Valley Fever and was at the point of death due to a misdiagnosis of his condition he was prescribed steroids, which immediately took him into a mental state that required much prayer and admittance to our county mental facility for a week, by God's grace has recovered and is again, his old self.

To say that I was thrilled at his statement that the President of the United States would one day come to our home, because we were going to start a new business of lending money to women in Kenya, and that he was going to complete his book to help finance the effort.

He went on with his usual passion about how we would eventually do the same thing in Bakersfield, as well as other places; especially his beloved East Saint Louis, Illinois, that he would write another book on how to redistribute wealth in America.

He vowed that we, with the help of God, would change the lives un-numbered thousands, of women and men by 2025. After learning that we would model our effort after The Grameen Bank in Bangladesh, we agreed that we would go ahead with plans to incorporate in Kenya.

We started with five women and have been able to touch the lives of thousands of women and their families. I have not gone to Kenya when he started this, but was blessed to go with him and Melvin Thomas in March of 2013 and met the people that I have come to love and cherish. We are scheduled to travel to Kenya in March 2016 and stay for ten days.

As I look back I realize that I would not be the person I am today had I not gone through the trials that life brings to all of us. They have shaped me, to be theme that I am. Finally, but not finally, I owe much to my Lord, my parents, and my husband for taking me on this wonderful journey that we call life.

At times it seems to be a repeat effort, with the same results, but I am convinced that with the help of God – our dreams to continue to help others will come true.

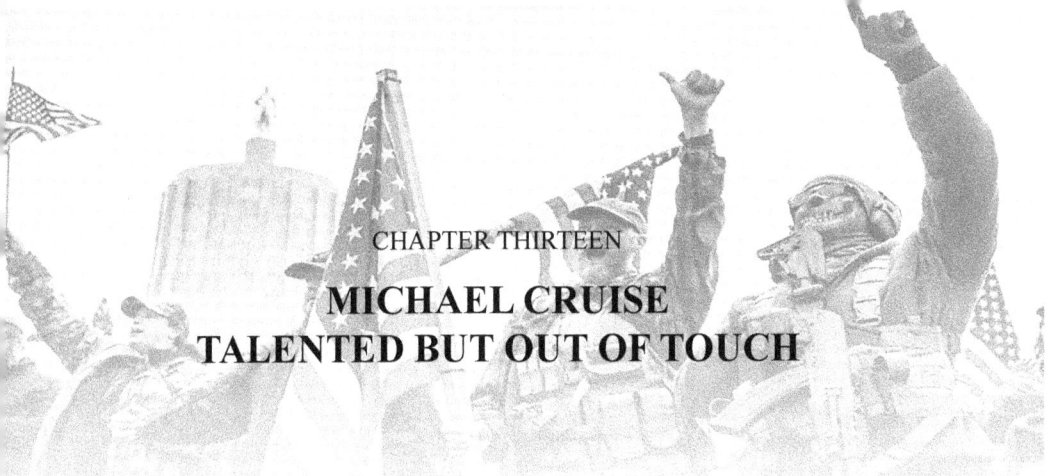

MICHAEL CRUISE
TALENTED BUT OUT OF TOUCH

I was born February 8, 1961, at Fort Hood, Texas, to Matthew and Cathryn Hicks-Cruise. I have an older brother Matthew Jonathan, and my sister Carmen, who passed away in May 2011. My father was a career military man and our family traveled the world on various military assignments.

My first memory was throwing rocks at chickens in Leesville, Louisiana, about the time President Kennedy was assassinated. The weather was cold, but we liked playing in the yard and running the chickens around the house and sometime under it. Although my father ran a tight ship, and still does, we were free to roam outside.

As I look back, I realize that I have always liked being outdoors, where my carefree spirit is able to spread it wings and sour into the heavens. As I grew older, I recall taking a trip with my family to New York to attend my mother's brother-in law's funeral. It was very interesting and exciting to travel through the South and hear my father talk about the Jim Crow South, about how bad it was to travel especially when traveling alone.

As fate would have it, our car broke an axle when we hit something on the highway. We were right outside a small town in South Carolina, on a Sunday morning. The tow truck driver called a repair shop and the owner opened his shop and repaired the problem in about four hours. Lesson one; there are some good people everywhere. When we returned home, we fell into our usual routine, I recall that we found a five dollar bill that had been torn, my brother Matthew J. taped it back together, and we had a sweet feast for two days.

When I was five, we traveled to Augsburg, Germany to be with our father, who had been there for six months. The trip on the ship was exciting when we were allowed on deck, but we spent most of the time in our cabin. We arrived in Frankfurt, and traveled to Augsburg by train. Talking about fast, the trains traveled at a very high rate of speed, and was always on time, as it came into the station, people scurried to get on, because they didn't stop but for a few minutes.

We were so happy to be reunited as a family; my father was the coordinator of the area that we stayed, because he was the highest-ranking enlisted man. That gave us a little status, but kept my father busy resolving disputes.

Six months later, I noticed that my mother was having panic attacks when she was around German people. She suffered a mental breakdown which resulted in our early return to the states, this time, leaving my father behind to finish his obligated tour of duty.

When we returned to the states by air, we returned to East Saint Louis and lived temporarily with my uncle Fred and his wife Burley. My mother was eventually committed to the county mental hospital in Alton, Illinois until my father was able to get reassigned on a compassionate reassignment. Just as we were getting into a routine, by this time we had moved closer to school, and lived with my grandmother Letha Wofford-Cruise-Brown.

Six months later, my father was appointed to the grade of Warrant Officer, and ordered to report to Fort Lee, Virginia for deployment to Vietnam. Just prior to his departure, I stuck a rusty nail in my foot, and for the first time I saw panic in his eyes, I later learned that my uncle James, my father's idol, had died from the same thing, because he was not administered a tetanus shot. He rushed me to the hospital as if I had been shot, and made sure that I received the shot. For the next three years, we saw him six times, and only for thirty days each time, before he was sent back to Vietnam.

We moved to a better neighborhood called Parkside, where a new school had been finished. Carmen asked to move to Atlanta with my father and his new wife. During school break, I went to Atlanta and was happy to see my father and Carmen.

I returned to East Saint Louis, and after a brief stay, I returned to Atlanta and enrolled into Therrell High School, which was five minutes from our house. After four years, my father and step-mother separated and later got divorced.

My father went to Bakersfield, California where my aunt Freda and my grandmother Letha had moved some years earlier. After many rounds of golf, he decided to seek employment. Carmen, and Matthew followed, and I came in time to finish my high school education, graduating in 1979 from Bakersfield High School, the home of the Drillers.

Carmen enrolled in the Registered Nursing Program and graduated near the top of her class. She worked for over thirty years and Kern Medical Center; she died from cancer in 2011. Just prior to her death, she was elected to the presidency of the local nursing union. Her death brought back memories that I could not shake. It was a difficult time for me because we were always close.

In 1980 I attended California State Bakersfield and lasted for one year, or shall I say survived for one year. My grades were less than what I was capable of doing; it was another tragic situation of not putting my life in order. I decided to move to Los Angeles in 1981 and got a job at The May Company, in their sales audit department. I enjoyed my job, and remained there for two and a half years. I had few if any goals, short or long term; I just worked and spent all of the money that I made.

I returned to Bakersfield in the summer of 1984, I experienced a "spiritual awaking", most of what I was learning wasn't anything that I had not heard before, but I realized that the Bible was the inspired word of God. With my newfound understanding I realized that I could depend on Jesus to help me unload my burdens.

I obtained several food services jobs, and after a year, my mother, who lived in New York, was having some problems with thugs in the neighborhood in which she lived. I decided to move to New York to help her. I went by bus that stopped in Las Vegas, instead of continuing on, I walked around the city, and was caught in a police sting operation.

My whole world turned upside down, I was convicted of burglary, and larceny from a person, and for carrying a knife. I was sentenced to thirty days, and three years of felony probation. After my release I was not allowed to leave the state.

I was welcomed into the home of the Fisher family, through the recommendation of Gene Fisher, a man who I met in jail. I found a job at the Las Vegas Hilton, and worked there for four years. It was about this time that I was introduced to rock cocaine, by the person who was instrumental in me getting the job at the Hilton. At first I used once every payday, and before long, I was hooked. My life and my value system was never the same until I found the Lord.

On the outside things seemed to be going alright, I continued working at the Hilton, and took another job at Western Linen. I rented an apartment and joined Saint James Missionary Baptist Church. After four months I met a woman there and we started drinking and using other drugs. Ultimately, I lost my second job and my apartment.

I lived from "pillar to post", until I was able to rent a room at the Daisy Hotel. I was released from probation and less than a month, I was back in jail for two counts of possession of a controlled substance. I was released in four and a half months, and placed back on probation for a period not to exceed six months.

I went back to work at the Hilton as a Banquet Stewart. I remained at the hotel that I rented in North Las Vegas for forty dollars a week. I continued working and began to sell marijuana, while still on probation.

The owner burned the hotel to collect insurance money. I was part of a class action suit and received seven hundred in cash. The Red Cross housed me for a month. I continued at the Hilton, and got another job at a pizza parlor; after a short time, I was promoted to line cook, it was there that I met my soon to be wife, Venus Bertha Boyd.

We began to live together and moved to a better one room apartment. We were both doing drugs on our off days, and weekends. Venus was thirty-eight when we met, and I was twenty-eight.

Venus got pregnant and stopped drinking and using drugs during her pregnancy. We got married a month before our first child was born. We were crushed when he was still born; we wanted to give him a name to honor his presence in the world, because I understood that when his body was formed, he also received a spirit, we named him Cornelius Secret Cruise.

Those were difficult days, although we stayed together, our marriage was never the same again. We continued to work and she rejoined me in drinking and drug use. Three months later, Venus got pregnant again, in 1989, we were blessed with the arrival of Mienna Star Cruise. She was born pre-maturely, and remained in Intensive Care for a month.

I continued working while Venus was looking for a job, things were difficult; we had a new baby and had to forgo drugs to feed her and buy diapers. On Easter Sunday, in 1990, I was arrested for attempted robbery and sent to prison for forty five months, and was placed on parole until 1996.

When I got out, Venus was gone. I returned to Bakersfield, and lived with my step-mother and my father. They told me that I would have to attend church with them, get a job, and could live with them for six months, at the end of the six months I would have to find an apartment.

I was so happy to see my family, it truly was overwhelming; my parents live in an exclusive part of town, and I had the run of the house. It was like heaven. They hired me with their company, Green Valley Landscaping. I made four hundred dollars each week, the most money that I had earned in a lone time. Times were good, but I was lonely. When the construction industry hit bottom, my parents had to close the business, and lay off seventy five people.

I got a job at the Fast Strip on Ming and Real Road, and since I was living on my own, I began to use drugs again. After realizing that the road that I was on was going to destroy me I started to attending church again, this time, with the determination to live right. I was taught the way of the Lord, and was baptized into Christ, for the second time, but continued to be around the same people that went around before I returned to church.

I stopped going to church about six months later. I enrolled in San Joaquin Valley College, and graduated with honors; I was awarded a certificate of completion in Business Administration. I was proud that I accomplished this while still working at the Fast Strip. The downside was my continued use of drugs.

I met a woman and moved her into to my apartment. I got another job at the Save U Food for about five months, and was fired because of theft. Shortly before I was to be released from my parole, I was violated for not reporting to my parole officer, and was returned to

Las Vegas, and was sent to prison for four months, the time I had remaining on parole.

I was ordered to a ninety day drug program and once again, did not finish and was returned to prison where I maxed out the original ten year sentence.

I returned to Bakersfield and stayed at the Bethany Mission, where I volunteered on the dorm crew. I worked odd jobs in town, and landed a real job at Gimmarra Vineyards as a line person in their bottling plant. I frequented the park on Baker Street, where I met Anthony Nellums, who later became my Brother in Christ.

My biological mother died in 1999, I was so distant from my relatives, because of my shame, my brother Matthew, had to find me to give me the sad news. Soon after her death, I was returned to prison because I was caught in a sting operation and pled guilty to the charge of being in possession of a controlled substance.

I did twenty-two month at the new Cochran substance abuse treatment facility. I was released in December 2001and placed on parole. A year later, I was arrested and convicted for second degree burglary and sentenced to another twenty two months. I was released to West Care Drug Program in 2004.

I later transferred to Legacy on "F" street in Bakersfield, and worked for my parents who were now licensed masonry and cement contractors. I was again blessed with a good job. My parents allowed me to move into a small house on the property where we stored our equipment. I was violated for not passing a drug test, and was assigned to an inpatient drug treatment program for a minimum of ninety days, where I remained another ninety days for a total of six months.

I got a job cleaning windows commercially, but failed another drug test and was placed into another drug treatment program. I was in an out of several programs, until I was released from parole in 2010. During a drunkard episode, I took a bad fall, and could not move. I spent four days in the hospital and sent to a rehabilitation hospital.

I got a job with Ralph Jennings installing energy efficient lighting in Northern California; after a slow down, I returned to Bakersfield and was brought into a business that my parents had started, and allowed a group of six people to have part ownership through sweat equity. All of us left the business without giving notice, we just left, leaving my parents with a total expenditure of twenty- five thousand dollars.

In spite of the outcome, they continue to help people out of poverty. I am amazed how they bounce back from what I call failure, but they view it as a learning experience, while making it through the day with, a renewed faith that God will send help, is success story. I work with my father doing anything that I can make a living on. I have my own apartment, and unconditional love and support from my mother and father.

I have recommitted my life to the Lord, and working on leaving my old crowd, and focusing on living a righteous life. I have hit many bumps in the road, but have not fallen into a hole of hopelessness. With the support of my church family, and the individual encouragement from my sisters and brothers, I am beginning to live an ordered and productive life. Pull Up From Poverty has created in me the hope and belief that I can be a productive part of society.

I am learning to think good thoughts, and live an ordered life, being led by the Spirit of God, and the people who have truly shown their love for me. I am determined to be part of the solution, and not part of the problem.

> I continue to work on me, and through study and faith in God, I am convinced that the revolving doors that I have passed through so many times, has been sealed. I look to the future with great anticipation and the realization that I am not along, and that my family loves me in spite of me.

UPDATE

After working in his family business for approximately two and a half years, he has returned to many of his old ways, but he has been released from parole, even though he has returned to many of his old ways. He currently help to manage a transitional house for men with mental and social problems many of whom are on parole.

RALPH JENNINGS STORY
Contributed by Ralph Jennings

My story is more than simply a story of urban survival; it serves as evidence that any person can overcome some of life's most debilitating challenges:

Childhood Sexual Abuse   *Poverty*
Destructive Self Image   *Alcohol/Drugs*
Sexual Addiction   *Rage/Violence*

Born in the month of March 1957 at Detroit city's Burton Mercy Hospital, I grew up a mixed baby (African-American, Native American, and French-Canadian) in one of Detroit's most notorious ghettos.

I was the oldest of six boys. My father was a 16+ year heroin junkie; and my mother was a beautiful, promiscuous, somewhat verbally abusive woman who was considered too "white" for black folks and too "black" for white folks!

At age 8, my parents divorced. Imagine the impact on an eight year old boy hearing his father tearfully tell him "...son *you have to be the man of the house now*". From that day, learning how to be a "MAN" became my consuming passion! And, I learned what being a man meant from the harsh streets of Detroit, Michigan during the 1960s and 70s!

But my life has also had its upside; and many fun times—Barbeques, Parties, Picnics, and Laughter. I experienced military life. I've obtained a college-level education. I once landed a really good job, received Christ as Savior (*though not yet as "Lord"*), and married a very beautiful woman – among other things.

Yet, my story also has a disturbing dark side. Blended with the seeming accomplishments, are seedy experiences a young person should not be exposed to and no human being should have to suffer through...

I was greatly influenced by Detroit's "Pimp/Player Culture". As a young boy, a couple of Detroit's prominent pimps and hustlers took me under their wing and I became like their 'adopted son'. These men controlled specific territories in Detroit's underworld, *owned* local police, politicians; and had names like "Hollywood", "Slim", and "Pretty".

They had grown fond of me and decided to teach me "the game" because they knew me as a "well-polished hustle machine". I was the youngster who ran to the store to buy cigarettes and cheap liquor for the gamblers at the local all-night after-hours spot. I would deliver newspapers in the morning before school, sell stolen sodas during school (*and eventually weed also*); and, shine shoes after school.

My mother was the only one who really understood this was simply my way of trying to "become a man". She did the best she could to discourage me from choosing this type of life. But it's hard for a young boy to hear the voice of reason over the sound of loud music, money, and laughter.

One of my close childhood friends was the oldest son of the lead singer for Motown's popular singing group - "The Four Tops". I once dated the daughter of Eddie Kendricks (*lead 1st tenor for Motown's "Temptations"*). I was one of only a few kids who had the pleasure of hanging out over at Smokie Robinson's home and later become closely associated with other Motown personalities like Rick James and El Debarge).

All of this gave me access to wealth, pleasure, power, and many willing and available women. And, I took advantage of it all! These women were willing to "pay" for the privilege to hang out near these personalities. And oh how willing they were! They'd pay in money and in many other ways.

By age 16, I had done it all. I was living with a 23-year-old woman as - the "man of the house". She was a beautiful asian/african-american, mixed woman who loved Billy Holliday and Etta James. She accepted my lifestyle, even allowing me have sex with other women in our home. Marijuana, Rum and Coca-Cola were always abundantly available. Fun was the order of the day, and I was determined to "fun" myself to death!

At age 17, however, I was inadvertently involved in a botched robbery attempt that resulted in the murder of a 13 year old paperboy. This experience traumatized me. It was unexpected and I was forced into position of protecting my cousin who foolishly committed the act.

Somehow, I secretly developed a destructive self-image as a result. I believe my sense of guilt over the boy's death, caused me to subconsciously condemned myself. Although I hid it well, my negative, guilty self-image began to dominate my actions and behavior. For years, I was completely unaware how much of my behavior was influenced by this fact.

To make matters worse, my promiscuous, "pimp/player" lifestyle slowly developed into a sexual addiction. Like Rick James, I became more and more involved in the sex industry - this ultimately devastated my life.

It produced two failed marriages, a criminal lifestyle of flesh-peddling, drug use, violence; as well as my fathering children who either didn't know me at all or who become completely bitter toward me.

It also resulted in my being arrested several times on sex-related and other offences related to this lifestyle. Finally, it resulted in my suffering more than 15+ years in prison!

MY TURNING POINT

During his final arrest, I was facing 125 years to life. I was arrested shortly after the enactment of California's new Three Strikes Law. This time, there were many misleading, false facts in the case; the bottom-line was, now I had a criminal history and facts or no facts the District Attorney was determined I was going to prison!

I was forced into accepting a plea agreement of 16 years at 80% in order to escape the possibility of facing a 125-year Life Sentence (*a few years later California Courts overturned this prosecutorial practice*). I now understand God's hand played a major role in what happened.

Deep inside, I knew I really was a child of God—even if I wasn't acting like one. I had simply lost my identity. The pleasures of sin blinded me from seeing the person I really was. I had forgotten the many supernatural encounters I had experienced over the years.

But, God had not forgotten me. And, God was determined I was going to remember Him again—and I would get my true identity back!

After a failed suicide attempt, I somehow conjured up the crazy idea of committing suicide—*a different way*. I said to God, sincerely from my heart:

> *"Just let me do something for you in prison, before I die. Please don't let me get out of prison, if it means straying away from you again. I'd rather live a short life and go to heaven, than live a long life and go to hell."*

I made a genuine, personal decision to take serious Jesus Christ's advice—"if you lose your life, you will save it…".I began waking up every morning with one primary goal— "**to live today as if it were my last**". I'd ask himself questions like "*What do you want to be found DOING WHEN YOU DIE?*", and living by words like those of the late, great Dr. Martin Luther King Jr. - "A man who's not willing to die for something, is not fit to live!"

Eventually, God made him a minister of the gospel while incarcerated. I maintained a reputation of being willing to **DIE for what I believed-GIVING BACK to God and man**. This commitment was tested many times. I have faced many death threats by dangerously violent men, gang-bangers, racists, even a few crooked cops!

I've been lied on, cheated, talked about, and mistreated! But God gave me victory through it all—REAL VICTORY!

For over a decade, I served as a spiritual leader for hundreds of incarcerated men. Twice, I was elected by the entire inmate population to represent their concerns before state officials and to settle disputes among them. I have been instrumental in preventing major prison riots, assaults, and murders.

I have received several commendations for my contributions from criminal justice/corrections professionals. I was one of only a very few inmates to receive a personal commendation from the prison Warden, Chief Deputy Warden, and Facility Captain at the California Correctional Institution.

Upon being released from prison, and after successfully completing my parole, I hired a man named Michael Cruise to help me work installing energy-efficient light fixtures throughout California. He admitted his personal struggle with drug use to me and I confided to him my intention to author a book. We were able to benefit each other during our time together.

On several occasions he would say "*I really think you should meet my dad. You talk just like him.*"

It would be almost a year after our last project together that the opportunity to meet his father (Matthew Cruise) finally presented itself. But Michael had been right! Our worldview and objectives was so similar it was uncanny. The more we talked the more we became convinced our paths had been divinely ordained to cross.

As he and I shared our goals and visions, the more convinced we became in "rightness" and timeliness of our cause – both from a spiritual and sociological perspective. My passion toward creating a tangible demonstration of what I call **God's Economic Love Culture** (i.e. The We Thing), simply provides a theological philosophy to the goals of Matthew and Barbara's "Pull Up From Poverty".

I have gladly joined with Matthew to produce what I believe is part of a 21st Century social "game-changer". Our efforts, like many others taking place all over the world, are part of a social evolution taking place with mankind. It is reminiscent of Jesus' statement "kingdom of God comes not with observation. (Luke 17:20-21)" Instead, it will occur inside the hearts of people and then - suddenly emerge upon the world scene!

My confidence and passion is at an all-time high. I now value the awesome, life-giving power of - "*giving back*"! I am convinced Matthew understands this even more than I. Together we both believe that God will provide a new corporate culture that will embrace our vision. In light of America's current economic realities (*brought about due to dishonest companies/practices operating in the traditional fashion*), we cannot remain so naïve as to unyieldingly trust only in the old traditional way of doing business.

A person in my situation is not supposed to make it - in the old traditional way of doing things. Almost all possible employment opportunities available to a person with my past and my educational level, is dismal at best!

Because of the real and tangible opportunity available to me through Pull Up From Poverty, my right to Life, Liberty, and the Pursuit of Happiness is no longer irrevocably hindered. Today, it is based solely upon my willingness to work hard and apply myself. I thank God for what is being accomplished through Pull Up From Poverty.

UPDATE

MR. JENNINGS CURRENTLY RESIDES IN TEXAS AND CONDUCTS A NATION WIDE POD CAST IN HIS ATTEMPT TO HELP PEOPLE BOTH PHYISCAL AND SPIRTUAL

CHAPTER FIFTEEN

WAYNE ANTHONY NELLUMS STORY

My name is Wayne Anthony Nellums; I was born April 14, 1960 in Little Rock, Arkansas. My parents were Willie Nellums and my mother name is Katherine Dotson-Nellums. There are twelve children in our family two of them have passed on". My mother was thirteen years old when she married my father. She completed the third grade and never returned to school. I had seven brothers and four sisters. My brother Charles is a police officer in Arkansas and my brother Willie passed away in 1997.

I started drinking hard liquor when I was eight years old; I could be "wasted" and no one would know it unless you got close enough to smell my breath. I would just go up and down the streets of Alzheimer, Arkansas and the men would give me whiskey to drink and laugh because I would stagger and fall; after a while, I could out drink them all.

My mother moved to a small town called Lonoke, Arkansas where I left high school after completing the eleventh grade. I left Lonoke and joined the Job Corps in Tulsa, Oklahoma. There I met a young woman who was full blood Indian and three months later, she was pregnant.

At first I was happy until she told me that her father lived on the Indian Reservation, and he did not like black people. I took to easy road and simply left the program. Since then I have tried to find her and I still wonder what happened to our child.

I returned to Lonoke in 1978 and stayed with my mother until she remarried - and my step-father told me to find another place to live. The only immediate place available to me at the time was to move in with my biological father.

He had not changed much; in fact he had grown worse. After three months, I moved to Indianola, Oklahoma, located near Lawton, Oklahoma. It was wildlife preservation and was the site the job corps in that area used. I obtained my General Education Diploma (GED) there. A year later I returned to Lonoke but this time my step-father was okay with my staying with them.

I enrolled at Shorter College in North Little, Arkansas I received an AA degree in Liberal Arts. Although I struggled and was a "C" average student, it was while attending this fine liberal arts school I met Thelma Miller and we had a daughter named Shauna. And since we were not married, Thelma gave our child her maiden name. Our daughter currently lives in Kansas City, Missouri and we have a healthy father and daughter relationship.

I enrolled into the University of Arkansas-Pine Bluff, where I received my BA Degree in Criminal Justice. I was on the dean's list for three straight semesters.

Thelma and I broke up. I met Danita Reed, a local girl who lived in Pine Bluff. We remained together for a year. During our relationship she also became pregnant, but I was informed that the child was not mine. When I asked her if it was true, she did not deny it, but commented "my aunt should not have told you."

I got a job with Lug by Emergency Service driving a taxi, tow truck, and on some occasions, I drove the ambulance. I worked there for three years until 1989 when I was beaten by three white men while a hundred or more people stood in a large circle cheering the fight on. When the police arrived they took everyone's statement, the men went home and I went to the hospital. I left against medical advice because I was biter and did not trust anybody. After over twenty years I have finally learned to trust a few people.

I enrolled at Pine Vocational in Pine Bluff, Arkansas and learned to drive eighteen wheelers. I landed a job driving for J. B. Hunt, I drove for Hunt and after six months changed employers and drove for Fryemiller Trucking, I lost my job because I had begun to abuse drugs again.

I found myself in Bakersfield, California on probation and unemployed. I hung around the park on Baker Street and reunited with the church of Christ when I met members of the Baker Street church of Christ during their homeless feeding ministry.

I was baptized again by their minister Isaac Sandifer, Jr. in 1993. I continued using drugs even though I was wearing the face of a Christian. Because I felt guilty I was in a constant battle with demonic forces even though I knew I was wrong I felt hopeless and without hope.

I was converted but not convicted, I was living with one foot in the church and one out of it, but most of my weight was on the foot that was leaning out of the church. Because of my mother's religious devotion when I was a child, I kept remembering the lessons that she had taught me, lessons that I had not revisited since I was a child, suddenly all came back to my memory.

The vision of hope initially appeared quite dim but I clung to the avenue of prayer, the last remaining life line before I would sink into a never-ending pit of despair and utter destruction. I began to pray to God for deliverance from this black hole. I began to pray out loud and asked God to deliver even as I was on my way to buy more drugs.

I was completely devastated and knew if God would not deliver me I planned to commit suicide right then and there, but I knew that, it would be the highest violation of the law of the very person that I was begging to deliver me.

About a block away from my drug source, I felt a release that removed the desire for drugs and as I turned around and looked heaven ward, I gave God the praise because I knew that it was He who had delivered me.

This deliverance was short lived, because I continued a pattern of being holy and unholy; I remained in the church even though I continued to abuse drugs and live a sinful life. I was slowly committing physical and spiritual suicide.

I was by then smoking crack cocaine, cigarettes and drinking booze every day. I supported my habit by doing odd jobs and when I lost total control, I began to rob people by strong arm tactics and intimidation of innocent people. But I was the one who was hurting the most.

I recall the only close call of going to jail, the day that I stole two bottles of Johnny Walker Red and later sold them to feed my habit. As I was leaving the store an alarm went off and I ran like I had never run before, I jumped a nearby fence crossed the freeway and began walking at a slow pace until I had cleared the immediate area. I decided then and there that I would never try to steal anything from a store again.

Although I was back in the church and on the surface I appeared to be alright, I was able to mask my true self from my early training after I became an alcohol abuser at a young age. I continued this horrific behavior pattern and began to enjoy the "art of the mark" I took great pleasure in outsmarting the next guy, especially if he appeared to have more than me. This erratic behavior acted as a safe haven to hide the terrible hurt that was always brewing inside if me.

After ten years of drug abuse I got tired of the lifestyle there was more hurt that you could ever imagine, the hurt that I inflicted on others and the personal hurt that I felt in the pit of my stomach. Again I started to remember the training that my mother taught me, it rang in my ears like a sounding cow bell. Her message was to never forget to pray and believe in Jesus and never give up.

I was awarded SSI-Social Security in nineteen ninety one based on my alcohol and drug related issues. This windfall allowed me to continue to abuse drugs and alcohol; I was cut off along with many others in 1998 only to be re-awarded in two thousand.

I was homeless for almost three years until I was placed in a program called Jail Link, where I was placed in the Royal Palm Hotel and again started receiving SSI Social Security. I was free of drugs while in Jail Link in September 2000. I started to attend the Brundage Lane church of Christ. After being clean and drug free I took a trip back home to Arkansas. After a week I returned to Bakersfield and met LaKeshia Olison, we were married three days later.

The first four months were great, I began to feel good about myself and our marriage but we began to stop communicating for reasons unknown to me and slowly began to grow apart, when she asked for a divorce, I was shocked, it happened as we were leaving the church. I am sure that she felt safer around men who appreciated her for what she was.

I attended the Bill Pickett Rodeo on a cool but pleasant Wednesday evening, when I returned home my wife of less than a year had packed and moved in with her female friend and they subsequently moved to Michigan. I was hurt and very upset. The only thing remaining in the house was a washer and dryer and a pet bird. I started to drink more each day which impaired my judgment. I began to drive while intoxicated and to spend endless days at my old safe haven, the park on Baker Street.

For the next three days I was in a drunken stupor. It was during this time that I met a young woman and we began to talk about our life experiences. We always had a bottle to drink, when we ran out I would go a purchase another one. I invited her to come to the house where we continued to drink until I took her back to the hotel that she was staying.

As we continued to talk, I was surprised to learn that she was the daughter of my wife's uncle. She returned to the house with me the next day, around noon she called her mother in San Pedro after she hung up she grew silent and withdrawn.

She was a completely different person. About an hour later she suddenly burst into tears and told me that her children were being abused and asked if I would drive her to San Pedro, California; we left Bakersfield around two o'clock in the afternoon and arrived in San Pedro around four thirty.

I parked in the rear parking area and waited while she went into her mother's apartment. It the day after the fourth of July and people were still setting off fireworks, and I did not hear the gun shots that were being fired less than fifty feet from me.

A few minutes later she returned with her children; during our return trip to Bakersfield, I noticed that she had a gun resting in her lap; I stopped the car and asked if she had injured anybody, and she said no

76

I just shot the place up. I took the gun and dropped it into the nearest trash can.

The following morning as I was eating breakfast, I noticed that the police had surrounded house. I went out and learned that I was being charged with kidnapping. I was dumbfounded when the police told me that the mother-in-law had custody of the children and I was an accomplice to several charges. I was faced with twenty years to life or was offered a plea bargain to serve nine years in prison. I did seven years and six months and was paroled back to Bakersfield.

I returned to church; this time fully committed to live a righteous life. I reacquainted myself with Brother and Sister Matthew and Barbara Cruise. They had started a program in Kenya to help women come out of poverty.

They knew that I did not have a job and asked if I would like to join them in a new business model where I would become a business owner by investing "sweat equity" I am now part owner in a business selling the best Bar Be Que in the world, I look forward with great anticipation to finally become a productive citizen by obtaining a loan from Pull Up From Poverty, in order to start my own business.

UPDATE

ANTHONY IS BACK DRIVING TRUCKS OVER THE ROAD WHILE TRAINING YOUNGER DRIVERS HE WILL JOIN US IN TRANSPORTING GOODS AND SERVICES IN THE SPRING OF 2023

UPDATE

MR NELIES CURRENTLY WORKS AN OVER "THE ROAD" DRIVER AND AN INSTRUCTOR FOR NEWLY LICENSE DRIVERS AND THE SAFETY OPERATIONS OF BIG RIGS. HE IS SCHEDULE TO BECOME A PARTNER IN HIS OWN BUSINESS BY PURCHASING HIS FIRST ELECTRIC RIG.

CHAPTER SIXTEEN

WHERE WILL THIS MONEY COME FROM

In 1990, the state of California deregulated the sale of gas. We formed a company to market natural gas to all customers who purchased the product through the Regulated Utility Companies. We had a large customer base, somewhere in the neighborhood of fifty million dollars per month. Due to our inability to obtain a promised line of credit, we had to close our business.

God has a sense of humor, because almost thirty years to the month, a black man from Bakersfield, California, walked into my small office located behind the walk-up restaurant, and said that he had been told that we might be able to join in an effort to change the environment.

He indicated that he had a patent, and need capital to get a third-party to verify his claim, by using a computer program, similar to the one used by car manufactures'. My wife and I became the first investors.

Even at this late stage of our Research and Development, I am bound by a Non-Disclosure Agreement not to divulge the name, or any information about the inventor, or the unit. I can say that our company, Pull Up From Poverty will be one of the flag ship entities in the marketing of the product that makes, and in a sense, we trap the force that produce electricity without being connected to the electrical grid.

Because our unit does not rely on the sun, wind, or geo thermal, and does not emit any carbon, only in the manufacturing of the actual unit, we will be able to claim what is known in a small circle as Carbon Credits. It is through the sales of these credits, world-wide, that we will amass a large sum of money, and redistribute it to the same world, starting here in Bakersfield. We faced ridicule, disbelief, and jeers. The statement used by people who have no desire to help in any way, is the great defense of "if I wouda cudda," as they utter the words, it sounds too good to be true, and the then the satisfaction that I get by asking "which part", because I finally learned that either they were not listing, or did not have the capacity to think beyond their circumstances.

We are thankful that our source is from God, in answer to the prayer that I uttered on my bed of affliction. As to often be the case, when men and women of color obtain money, the word in the street is "you know they are selling drugs".

I have finally discovered that I am a drug addict, I am, and continue to be addicted to giving. This is not a sudden inspiration from above, nor is it a try at being cute, because as cavalier as it may sound, the truth is, like most drugs, it almost destroyed my family. Even in this most God like act, you have to use wisdom, and not get ahead of God.

CHAPTER SEVENTEEN

POVERTY –A BATTLE THAT WE WILL WIN

Technology and the use of existing infrastructure have revolutionized the way business is conducted, nationally and internationally. Other countries are starting to do business in the streets of America through various methods of providing goods and services all over the world.

In our existing financial crisis and political unrest many who would not accommodate the idea of anything other than the traditional method of providing these services are now accepting and applying these new business models, to pull people out of poverty.

Our government, through their antiquated way of providing goods and services, coupled with the trend of outsourcing everything imaginable, has left the poor and working poor at the brink of destruction. It is no longer is it a struggle between classes and, races; or, the rich against the poor, we are now in a struggle to maintain the lifestyle many have taken for granted, rich or poor.

We are embarking on a new frontier, one in which technology is almost as valuable a piece of prime real estate or stock. It is environmentally friendly, with no threat to human life or wildlife. It is easier to maintain than an acre of land in Jasper County, Mississippi in eighteen sixty-six!

This new system of obtaining capital is accessible to any citizen who has the same spirit as our founding fathers. A view that President Lincoln saw amid one of the most challenging periods in the history of this great nation. This vision would place a silver spoon in the mouth of any person who shares the hopes and dreams of our founding fathers.

To help us remember, you should carefully read the Gettysburg Address, presented at the dedication to those who gave their lives for this great American Dream. I recited this speech as a young boy during the eighth grade graduation ceremony so many years ago. I have had to go back and learn it again, and not just to learn it, but to be a participant in that dream.

One of the Organizations that I worked with in the past, The Concerned Leaders of the Community, Of Bakersfield, started a contest regarding this speech among a group of young boys in the third and fourth grade at McKinley Elementary School in my hometown of Bakersfield, California.

The winner was to be given an all-expense paid trip with their family to Disneyland. We did not complete the contest, because of some internal issues the organization; but I believe if it had effected one boy, as it did me, it will be worth every dollar.

Your mental rite of passage, to the unfolding of a new way to remove people from poverty is to know, not memorize this great oratorical document.

I suggest that you simply write it out and read it seven times a day for seven days. You will know it just like you know your date of birth. At first it might seem impossible, but hang in there, the prize is a new awareness of what this great country can and must do.

For your convenience we have provided you with this famous speech at the beginning of this book. It gave hope to many who dared not to hope; it is in its original format; including the emphasis and stops delivered on that great day in history.

CHAPTER EIGHTEEN

MIRACLES

BY PERMISSION OF RANDALL BREWER

James 5:15 says, "And the prayer of faith will save the sick, and the Lord will raise him up." Faith comes by hearing so, if you want to get healed, focus on what you're hearing. Luke 5:15 says, "Then the report went around concerning Him all the more; and great multitudes came together to hear, and to be healed by Him of the infirmities." These people came to hear and, as a result of their hearing, they were healed. Faith is the determining factor but many people are too busy to do the one thing that causes faith to come. They'd rather go shopping or work in their garden than to sit down and hear the preaching of the Word. These are the people who remain sick and many times die an early death. They are interested in healing but not hearing. They want the preachers to stop talking so much and hurry up and lay hands on them. Little do they know that without the Word their body and their spirit deteriorate by the minute. It affects every living cell in your body. It is rich and it is powerful. It is medicine to all your flesh (Prov. 4:20). When you hear the Word healing power is at work inside of you. (The application of this principle is astonishing when you analyze where and how man was created, we came from the soil, the seed was the spoken word of God that germinated when God breathed into man, and man became a living soul).

"Now He was teaching in one of the synagogues on the Sabbath" (Luke 13:10). Jesus was teaching making it possible for faith to come. The Bible is spiritual food and healing medicine and there is no word of God that is void of power. It is rich in light and spiritual nutrition and life for all your flesh. Any time the Word is preached, taught, or read there is life coming out of it. "And behold, there was a woman who had a spirit of infirmity eighteen years, and was bent over and could in no way raise herself up" (vs. 11). The word "infirmity" means

82

'weakness' and notice that this was a "spirit" of infirmity. She has a spirit of weakness that had her bent over where she couldn't stand up. Satan did this to this woman and in vs. 16 Jesus called this woman's problem satanic bondage. It makes one wonder why some people call sickness a blessing in disguise and that God uses sickness to teach them something. It is total and complete foolishness to think this way. God teaches through the Word, not through cancer and heart disease. Sickness is the work of the devil (Acts 10:38) and until you get that settled in your heart and mind you cannot have faith to be healed and made whole.

Sickness and disease weaken you and it would have been easy for this woman to stay home in bed and not go to the synagogue that day. She had every excuse to stay home and not go but she went anyway. Not long after she was front and center listening to every word Jesus had to say. In your weakness God's strength is revealed. He told Paul, "my grace is sufficient for you, for my strength is made perfect in weakness" (2 Cor. 12:9). The Message Bible says, "My strength comes into its own in your weakness." People who magnify God don't have a problem with the devil. It's those who stay home and ignore the hearing of the Word of God that get sick, stay sick, and leave this planet before they're supposed to. These are the people who don't know what God's will is and don't realize that faith begins where the will of God is known. This woman was frozen in a bent over condition for eighteen long uncomfortable years but still she found a way to go to the synagogue and hear the preaching of the Word of God. This made her a candidate for a miracle.

When God planned out your life He laid out everything you'll need to fulfill your destiny. Ps. 31:19 (NIV) says, "How abundant are the good things that you have stored up for those who fear you that you bestow in the sight of all, on those who take refuge in you." Promotion, increase, and divine health is stored up for you. The Message Bible says, "What a stack of blessing you have piled up for those who worship you, ready and waiting for all who run to You to escape an unkind world." In 1 Sam 16 the prophet Samuel filled his horn with oil to anoint one of Jesse's sons to be the next king of Israel. All the elder sons passed before Samuel but only David got anointed with the oil. What God has stored up for you can go to nobody else. It's got your name on it for it already belongs to you. When you honor God with integrity and excellence these blessings will follow after you wherever you may go. What God started in your life He is going to finish? What He promised you He will bring to pass. What you can't do on your own God will make happen for you.

When you honor God blessings will chase you down and overtake you. God is an overflow God and what He has planned for you is bigger than you can think or imagine. When the dark clouds of sickness and disease come rolling in don't get discouraged and think the rain of calamity will fall on you. Just because it's the flu season does not mean you have to succumb to it like everybody else. Just because cancer and heart disease runs in your family does not mean you have to roll over and play the victim to these fatal diseases also. No, above every dark cloud is the sunshine of divine health, prosperity, and having a sound mind. Doctors don't have the final say, God does. (My doctor told me on January 2, 2000, that I had six months to live, guess what, in twenty four days it will be 2023, "you do the math)".He can part those clouds just like He parted the Red Sea and rays of healing, favor, and promotion will shine on you. One touch of God's favor can thrust you to the next level. In one moment you can be made well, all your bills can be paid off, and you can meet the person of your dreams. Do your part and get in agreement with God. Start acting like it's going to happen. When you do that you also will become a candidate for a miracle.

"But when Jesus saw her, He called her to Him, and said to her, 'Woman, you are loosed from your infirmity'" (Luke 13:12). Jesus did not say, "Woman, get ready. I am about to set you free." No, He said she was loosed now, not going to be. Is she still physically bent over? Yes, she is, but this is a vital part of faith. You must believe you are loosed and set free before you see the manifestation of it. Luke 4:18 says Jesus was anointed "to preach deliverance to the captives" and "to set at liberty those who are oppressed." This woman had been in bondage and robbed of her strength and ability to live a full, productive life. Jesus announced to this woman, "You are free! You are released from your weakness! You are rid of your illness! You are liberated

84

from your trouble! You are loosed from your infirmity!" She is still bent over but Jesus said she was loosed. This is what faith is all about. Don't look at what you can see for faith looks at the unseen. Faith calls your bills "paid in full" even when you don't know where the money will come from. Faith calls you "free" even when it looks like you're still bound. ("Don't judge a book by its cover)".

Jesus said in Matt. 6:22, "The lamp of the body is the eye. If therefore your eye is good, your whole body will be full of light." When you have an attitude of faith that pure eye is letting sunshine into your life. With an attitude of expectancy you can believe those dark clouds of defeat and mediocrity will roll away and that God will bring into your life everything you need to be made whole and to fulfill your destiny. God can make something good happen in a fraction of time that normally could take years to accomplish. Time means nothing to God. To Him a day is as a thousand years and a thousand years as a day (2 Peter 3:8). If your forecast looks depressing then believe God and the Son will shine in your life. Weeping may last for the night but joy comes in the morning (Ps. 30:5). When some people are hurting they may believe that being blessed by God is like finding a needle in a haystack. The good news is that God owns the haystack and He knows where all the blessings are at. He is more than capable of bringing those blessings of wholeness into your life. He controls the clouds and when darkness overtakes the righteous the light of your breakthrough will come bursting in.

"And He laid His hands on her and immediately she was made straight, and glorified God" (Luke 13:13). The works of the devil glorify the devil whereas the works of God glorify God. It warms the heart of God when you know He wants to be good to you. There is a freedom that comes with knowing you've been accepted and approved by the great God of the universe. You don't have to walk around burdened with insecurities wondering if God loves you or not. You can have peace of mind knowing that He loves you so much that He sent His only begotten Son to die for you and on that cross provision was made for every need you'll ever have. If you're hurting then rejoice because pain is a sign of new birth. It's always darkest just before the dawn. In the midst of his difficulty Job said, "For I know my Redeemer lives"

(Job 19:25). Trust God to take care of you. His purpose for your life is bigger than you can imagine and He won't let any problem overtake you that you're not able to handle. Rest assured that if some trial would keep you from your destiny God would never allow it to happen. Don't sink in the mire of self- pity but get ready for restoration to come into your life. In the end Job came out with twice as much as he had before.

The ruler of the synagogue was heated and had much grief over what happened. He was upset because Jesus had healed on the Sabbath and with indignation he said to the crowd, "There are six days on which men ought to work; therefore come and be healed on them, and not on the Sabbath day" (Luke 13:14). You have got to be influenced by the devil to get mad when a woman who's been bent over for eighteen years gets set free. Traditionally, religious people who don't know God are the meanest people on the planet. They'll beat you and kick you and then give you a scripture to justify what they did. They are heartless. They have a form of godliness but deny the power thereof (2 Tim. 3:5). Jesus answered him and said, "Hypocrite! Does not each one of you on the Sabbath loose his ox or his donkey from the stall, and lead it away to water it?" (vs. 15). Thirsty donkeys should be watered and bound people should be loosed. It takes the devil and confused theologians to say they don't know if you should water the donkey or not. This woman was a daughter of Abraham (vs. 16) and this means she was a daughter of faith, of covenant. She ought to be loosed no matter what day it is. "And when He said these things, all His adversaries were put to shame; and all the multitude rejoiced for all the glorious things that were done by Him" (vs. 17).

Jesus said in Luke 12:32, "Do not fear, little flock, for it is your Father's good pleasure to give you the kingdom." Nothing brings God more joy than to see you flourish and become all you were created to be. He created you to excel and take new ground for the kingdom. God wants to show you the greatness of His power and He has put His favor on you so you could accomplish what you couldn't do on your own. Ps. 5:12 says, "For You, O Lord, will bless the righteous; With favor You will surround him as with a shield." Everywhere you go you've got an advantage, a divine empowerment that causes new doors to be opened that couldn't be opened before. The prophet Isaiah takes it a step further when he says, "Arise, shine; For your light has come! And the glory of the Lord is risen upon you" (Is. 60:1). The word "glory" means 'a heavy favor' with the emphasis being on the weight. The prophet is saying you are weighed down with God's goodness. It is heavy upon you. It will cause you to pray bold prayers and believe for the extraordinary. When you know you are heavy with favor you will arise and this is when God will cause you to shine. You'll step into a new level of your destiny.

Many are heavy with worry, disappointment, sickness, and lack but you are heavy with the favor and goodness of God. You are heavy with joy and new opportunities. You are heavy with explosive blessings where you can pay your house off and rise up off that bed of sickness. Shake off the doubt and discouragement and rise up with a new perspective. You don't have ordinary favor or just enough favor. No, God has touched your life with heavy favor. You'll think big and ask big because you'll expect God's favor in a new way. Joshua was once in a battle and nightfall was approaching. He asked for the sun to stand still and it did for three hours. That is heavy favor when the entire planet stops spinning because you asked it to. When you believe that you have heavy favor you know that God has the final say in whatever happens in your life. You know that healing and restoration is coming your way. That what is broke will be mended and that what is lost will be found. Dreams will come to pass and destinies will be fulfilled. Be like Joshua and ask God to do something out of the ordinary. You have heavy favor and this is your time to rise and shine. God is ready to take you somewhere you've never been before.

Every person who ever came to Jesus to get healed, got healed. There were no exceptions. Jesus was and still is in the healing business. A lot of people think Jesus healed them on His own but He openly declared that it was their faith that did it. Their faith made them a candidate for a miracle and it was their faith that healed them. God is no respecter of persons (Acts 10:34) and if their faith made them whole, your faith will make you whole. Luke 17:11,12 tells how one day Jesus was traveling to Jerusalem. He is not teaching nor is He having a healing service. He is traveling. He passed through a small village and ten lepers yelled at Him from a distance. They stood afar off because leprosy was a terminal disease which brought with it a social death sentence. They had to separate themselves and could no longer associate with other people (Deut. 5:2; Lev. 13:45,46). They couldn't be with their family nor could they work. Their lives were essentially over and all they could do was live secluded lives and wait for this dreaded disease to end their life with much pain and suffering.

"And they lifted up their voices and said, 'Jesus, Master, have mercy on us!'" (Luke 17:13). They desired a healing but asked for mercy. God is called "the Father of mercies and God of all comfort" (2 Cor. 1:3) and Ps. 86:5 says, "For You, Lord, are good, and ready to forgive, and abundant in mercy to all those who call upon You." Grace and mercy are freely given but must be received by faith. Jesus answered them and said, "Go show yourselves to the priests" (vs. 14a). You only do this if you are healed (Lev. 13,14). It's the priest who proclaims the leper is cleansed and releases him back into society. You don't want to go see him if you're not healed. These are the same priests who crucified Jesus. You could be stoned to death if you went to the priest and still had leprosy. When Jesus told them to go show themselves to the priests they were not yet clean. They still had leprosy. The lepers didn't question Jesus. They didn't try to reason it out and they didn't walk by sight. They just turned around and began to walk in the direction of the priest. "And so it was that as they went, they were cleansed" (vs. 14b).

These ten lepers came to Jesus so they had faith He could heal them. The Lord gave them instructions and they did what He told them to do. Faith obeys. Faith acts on the Word. When did they get healed? Then and there? No, they got healed as they went to see the priest. Many people don't believe they're healed until they see the manifestation and get a good report from the doctor. There is no faith in saying, "I'll believe it when I see it." Were these lepers healed when Jesus sent them to the priest? No! You've got to believe you're healed no matter how you feel and no matter what the symptoms tell you. Jesus said go to the priest so they went. Faith is an action and as they went they were acting like they were cleansed. They were acting like they had a right to go see the priest. They acted on the Word and as they did they were healed. Sad to say, only one of the ten came back to thank

Jesus and glorify God. Where were the other nine? Why weren't they thankful? When God does something good for you, give thanks. Let others know what God did for you. Jesus looked at the man and said, "Arise, go your way. Your faith had made you well" (vs. 19).

The King James Bible and other translations say that Jesus told the man, "Your faith has made you whole." The other nine were healed but this man was made whole. The nine who were non-thankful no longer had leprosy but their body still bore the marks of what was eaten away by this dreaded disease. The one man who came back and glorified God, however, had all his missing skin and fingers and other limbs restored to a better condition than what they were before. He was made whole and in his body there was nothing missing and nothing broken. He became a "no lack" person. Ps. 34:9,10 says, "Oh, fear the Lord, you His saints! There is no want to those who fear Him. The young lions lack and suffer hunger; But those who seek the Lord shall not lack any good thing." Deep down inside you have to know that because you trust in the Lord you also are a "no lack" person. He has given you all things that pertain to life and godliness (2 Peter 1:3). He has breathed His life into you and He has equipped and empowered you to fulfill your destiny. You are well able to become the person God intended you to be.

God's favor is upon you so you must see yourself as a "no lack" person. How you see yourself determines how you will live your life. Prov. 23:7 says, "For as he thinks in his heart, so is he." See yourself healthy, wealthy, and wise. See yourself being told by God, "Well done, good and faithful servant." Your dream is not too big. You have the power, ability, determination, and perseverance to rise up and do what God has called you to do. You will never rise any higher than the image you have of yourself. If you see yourself lacking in some area it will set limits on how far you can go in life. Know and believe that you are not average. You are not ordinary. Your maker is the creator of the universe and He put in you everything you need to perform at the highest level. He has crowned you with His favor that will allow you to overcome any obstacle, to accomplish your God given dream. You are a "no lack" person. Victory is in your DNA. Almighty God has infused strength, talent, value, and confidence in you. Your dream may look impossible but you are equal to it. There is no obstacle too big for you, no dream too great.

You have been armed for battle so have a warrior mentality. You are "strong in the Lord and in the power of His might" (Eph. 6:10). God is strong and He wants you to be strong. Be like David who was born to defeat Goliath. When he heard the giant taunting the people of Israel he was in fact hearing his destiny calling out to him. He could have run away like all the rest but in his heart there was this image of God that said, "The Lord is my shepherd; I shall not want" (Ps. 23:1). He was saying, "I know I am a 'no lack' person." In the natural the giant was much bigger than David but scripture says David ran toward Goliath. He knew God was on his side. He knew he would come behind in no good thing (2 Cor. 1:7). He didn't face the giant in his own power and might but rather in the strength of the Lord. The King of kings and Lord of lords was by his side. When you run toward your giant God will make a way where there seems to be no way. He will help you accomplish what you could not do on your own.

The size of your battle indicates the size of your future. The giant Goliath was an indicator that David would one day be king. When obstacles arise in your life don't run away in doubt, fear, and frustration. No, rise up and rejoice. Run to your giant because this means you've got a bright future ahead of you. Goliath was not put in David's path to defeat him, he was put there to promote him. No weapon formed against you shall prosper (Is. 54:17). What the enemy means for evil, God means for good (Gen. 50:20). Promotion, increase, and new levels of favor are waiting for you on the other side of your giant. Don't run from your obstacle, run toward it. If you want to defeat the lion in your life you must run to the roar, not away from it. God is on your side and Paul said in 2 Cor. 4:16 (MSG), "So we're not giving up. How could we? Even though on the outside it often looks like things are falling apart on us, on the inside, where God is making new life, not a day goes by without His unfolding grace." When you face your enemy like David did you'll come out ahead and better than you were before.

Just prior to the Lord's triumphant entry into Jerusalem He and the great multitude that followed Him came to Jericho. On the road just outside the city blind Bartimaeus and a fellow blind companion sat on the road begging. "And hearing a multitude passing by, he asked what it meant. So they told him that Jesus of Nazareth was passing by" (Luke 18:36,37). Good things start to happen when you hear about the good things of God. Immediately Bartimaeus responded by crying aloud, calling Jesus by name, "Jesus, Son of David, have mercy on me!" (Mark 10:17). God is rich to all who call upon Him and Rom. 10:13 says, "For whoever calls upon the name of the Lord shall be saved." They must have heard about Jesus for why else would they get so excited when He passed by? They heard that Jesus went about doing good and healing those who were oppressed of the devil because God was with Him. They must have heard about the man with the withered hand and the woman with the issue of blood. These blind men called on Jesus to have mercy on them. How could they call on Him, on whom they didn't believe? They would not have called on Him unless they had faith that He could heal them.

If you have faith, you call out. You reach out, you step out of the boat. If you don't have faith you don't do anything. Unbelief won't call on the Lord. Unbelief sits and says there is no use. Why try? Why go on? They believe their situation is hopeless and ask. "What's the use?" These people do not call on the name of the Lord and for them there is no healing or deliverance. These two blind men cried out for healing mercy and the crowd rebuked them and warned them to be quiet. You would think the crowd would have supported them but they didn't. Mark 10:48 says Bartimaues cried out even louder, "Son of David, have mercy on me!" When he called out Jesus stopped. Calling out gets the Lord's attention. He stopped because they called. He heard their faith. This would not have happened had they not called. Jesus would have continued to walk on by. "So Jesus stood still and commanded him to be called. They then called the blind man, saying to him, 'Be of good cheer. Rise, He is calling you'" (vs. 49). People are fickle. The same crowd that told him to be quiet were now encouraging him to go to Jesus.

"And throwing aside his garment, he rose and came to Jesus" (Mark 10:50). Here was faith in action. This was no ordinary garment. This garment was issued by the governing authorities signifying that he was legitimately blind thus giving him a legal right to beg for his daily necessities. By throwing aside his garment Bartimaeus was saying he knew he would soon be a beggar no more and thus became a candidate for a miracle. Jesus stopped and commanded the man to be brought to Him. He asked "What do you want Me to do for you?" (vs. 51). He did not tell Bartimaeus and his companion what to believe for, they had to tell Him. What should you believe for? It's not up to God, it's up to you. It's according to your faith and what you can believe for. You ask for what you can confidently expect to receive. The man said, "Lord, that I may receive my sight." Then Jesus said to him, "Receive your sight; your faith has saved you" (Luke 18:42). Jesus gave him exactly what he said he wanted to receive. No more, no less. This is what he had faith for. You receive according to the ability of your faith.

God has been good to everybody. His favor has been manifested in the lives of every person who has ever been born. The very fact that you are alive and breathing is a testimony that God's favor has been poured out in your life. The good news is that as time draws to a close His unprecedented favor will be poured out to a greater degree than it's ever been before. Eph. 2:7 says "that in the ages to come He might show the exceeding riches of His grace in His kindness toward us in Christ Jesus." We are now living in the "ages to come" that Paul was talking about. He was saying that he saw limited power but you will see unlimited power. You will see the unsurpassing greatness of God's goodness. The NLT Bible says, "So God can point to us in all future ages as examples of the incredible wealth of His grace and kindness toward us, as shown in all He has done for us who are united with Christ Jesus." The word "unprecedented" means 'unmatched, unparalleled, for the first time.' What you will see in your life will be bigger, greater, and better than anything you've ever seen before. He will show you His goodness in ways you've never seen before.

Words give life to your faith so openly declare that God's favor is upon you and working in your life. When you do that you step out of the natural and into the supernatural. To reach your highest potential you will need doors opened that you cannot open on your own. This is when God's favor comes into play in your life. If you will believe this God will take you higher and farther than you ever thought possible.

God will do something astounding, remarkable, overwhelming, and breathtaking. You serve an awesome God who will do awesome things in your life. Awesome is the opposite of ordinary. What you'll see in your future will supersede what you've seen in your past. God has favor that is unparalleled, promotions that are astounding, good breaks that are remarkable. You will be amazed at all the good things that God has in store for you. All that He's done before will pale in comparison to what He's about to do for you. Believe that something awesome is coming your way. Don't look for the ordinary but expect the extra ordinary. Expect God to do something you've never seen before.

CHAPTER NINETEEN

FROM BANKRUPTCY TO A BILLIONAIRE IN FIVE YEARS

You have just read some very interesting information taken from the Bible. On December 9, 2022. My chapter seventh Bankruptcy was discharge is defined as "the state of being completely lacking in a particular quality or value. Moral bankruptcy of turning away desperate people even though people in power can retrieve them. In 2021 I was scheduled to initiate a war on poverty through a system founded by Dr. Muhammad Yunus. No pun intended, we were trapped from progressing by the COVID Virus. The timing of revenue verses income was thrown into the trashcan of fate. We lost everything including the will to continue. I stayed in bed for three months, in a highly depressed state. Due to the fact that we were a start-up company, all of the overhead was put in my name; causing a rift between me and my wife that we continue to try and repair. In order to start over and to get relief from our debtors, as a community property state my wife and I had to declare bankruptcy. So you may ask how can you go bankrupt one year, and claim to become a billionaire at the end of the following year. I am glad you asked, the sale of a bio stimulant call Symbiosis AGx. Ain't God xellent. Upon observation you might say it is a miracle. Someone once said that if you want to start a successful business, you must find something that people view as a necessity, and they buy, use, and buy again. They thought that toilet paper fit the description. I might argue that AGx is also in that category in the area of farming. Humans need food, in an attempt to satisfy that need, humans have destroyed the capacity for the earth to produce healthy food without the use of pesticides, herbicides, and non-organic additives that has not only destroyed the bacteria needed for the soil to reach its full potential in the natural process, while at the same time began a spiral that will enhance global warming, and the destruction of the earth. AGx is almost a miracle, but not quite. Several independent agencies have agreed that AGx will become the "rock star" of the farming community world-wide, because it will increase yield between 16-26%, reduce irrigation requirements by 50-66 percent, while reducing the need for federalizer, herbicides and pesticides. Wow!!!

We own a company in Kenya called IIRAD, LTD, or the International Institute for Research and Agricultural Development, LTD. We also own The California Agricultural Biostimulant Cooperative, LLC, located in Bakersfield, California.

Information to identify the case:

Debtor 1	MATTHEW CRUISE	Social Security number or ITIN	xxx-xx-6529
	First Name Middle Name Last Name	EIN __-_____	
Debtor 2 (Spouse, if filing)	BARBARA CRUISE	Social Security number or ITIN	xxx-xx-0114
	First Name Middle Name Last Name	EIN __-_____	

United States Bankruptcy Court   Eastern District of California

Case number: 22-11316

Order of Discharge

12/15

IT IS ORDERED: A discharge under 11 U.S.C. § 727 is granted to:

MATTHEW CRUISE   BARBARA CRUISE
dba BAKERSFIELD ISLAND ASSOCIATION ,
dba UP AND ATAM MAINTENANCE , fdba
FRESH START HOUSE

12/12/22   By the court: Rene Lastreto II
                                        United States Bankruptcy Judge

Explanation of Bankruptcy Discharge in a Chapter 7 Case

This order does not close or dismiss the case, and it does not determine how much money, if any, the trustee will pay creditors.

Creditors cannot collect discharged debts

This order means that no one may make any attempt to collect a discharged debt from the debtors personally. For example, creditors cannot sue, garnish wages, assert a deficiency, or otherwise try to collect from the debtors personally on discharged debts. Creditors cannot contact the debtors by mail, phone, or otherwise in any attempt to collect the debt personally. Creditors who violate this order can be required to pay debtors damages and attorney's fees.

However, a creditor with a lien may enforce a claim against the debtors' property subject to that lien unless the lien was avoided or eliminated. For example, a creditor may have the right to foreclose a home mortgage or repossess an automobile.

This order does not prevent debtors from paying any debt voluntarily or from paying reaffirmed debts according to the reaffirmation agreement. 11 U.S.C. § 524(c), (f).

Most debts are discharged

Most debts are covered by the discharge, but not all. Generally, a discharge removes the debtors' personal liability for debts owed before the debtors' bankruptcy case was filed.

Also, if this case began under a different chapter of the Bankruptcy Code and was later converted to chapter 7, debts owed before the conversion are discharged.

In a case involving community property: Special rules protect certain community property owned by the debtor's spouse, even if that spouse did not file a bankruptcy case.

For more information, see page 2 >

Official Form 318   **Order of Discharge**   page 1

CHAPTER TWENTY

PEOPLE ON THE TRAIN

On November 2, 2022 I left Bakersfield, California. My wife Barbara had a quick lunch after church. Barbara who is a retorted registered nurse, did not feel comfortable with me traveling more than forty-three hours by bus and train to Los Angeles to St Louis, Missouri, as most eighty-three year old men can attest to, when you "gotta go, you gotta go". Upon my return to where my one luggage was, she was talking to a man, Pastor Magnus Chrostopher and ask him to "look out" for me. I thank him for his help and support. I was on the train, or waiting in a train or bus station for a total of fifty-three hours. I talked to approximately eighty people. My story was the same, the test, followed by my disclaimer, and continued to get to know them and tell them a little about me. My task was made easier because I was wearing my cap that said "Korea War Veteran. Many would say "my grandfather served back in that war. (Sure know how to make a guy feel old). I will list as many as I can recall, but will highlight those who texted me later, or committed to stay in touch with me. Michael and Heather Branscom and his mother Karen, work as an IT manager for a Danish firm. (Just what we need. I attempted to convince him to join our firm. To maintain his privacy, I will just say that he has made his decision but the door is still slightly open. You remember the test we took earlier, Patricia K. Horton, Retired marine Master Sergeant who became my sponsor in doTerra a multi-level marketing company that promote herbal medicine. She was a "hoot", and in spite of a limp, she helped me with my carry-on items. Armando Marquez, conductor on the Amtrak, due to the stress of waiting we did not get off on a right footing, but was able to talk sensibly, and continue to stay in touch. And finally but not over, Kristi Kish from Rock Port, Missouri her response per our meeting in the train station, Dear Mr. Cruise, I want to thank you for blessing us with your stimulating conversation which helped that boys and I to pass the time waiting for the delayed train last night. It was great to see my nephew interact with someone other than family, and you blessed him with new ideas that he has never let himself think about. I was also blown away to run across someone that knew of the Bondo, Kisumu and our family's village area.

I do pray that God blesses the remainder of your journey and that you get home safely to your beautiful wife soon.

We continue to development a relationship with this family.

Although I met at least fifty people who I personally talked with, the highlight of my trip was meeting Mary Louis Randle; she had been released from prison for violating parole, who was returning to Kansas City Missouri; after observing her and two other people, who appeared to be together, that they had not eaten, I gave each of them forty dollars, the couple never returned by Mary did, we promised to stay in touch when the left the train in Kansas City, and to my surprise, she called me after of returned home needing money to find a place to live, because it was freezing. She found a room that the owner rented to her for four hundred dollars per month, I was short on cash and the new landlord agreed to take half; which I sent to her. A few days later the landlord threatened to put her out because she "had bills to pay". You guessed it I sent her the money, but not without drams, Western Union refused to release the money because I fit the profile of a person who commit fraud. I had to get a refund, and when I went to another vendor, I learned that one entity protects western union, money gram, Walmart to Walmart, and I had to get an associate to send the money.

She reported to her parole officer and has found a job making fifteen dollars an hour, and will be moving into her own apartment. I referred her to the Downtown church of Christ in Kansas City, and indicated that there were no strings attached, she said "Mr. Cruise, all that you have done to help me, I will go wherever you say".

CHAPTER TWENTY-ONE

THE AFTER ACTION REPORT
THE PULL UP FROM POVERTY HALL OF FAME

Hosea Tindle (Posthumous) His saying "When You Know better, you ought to do better". A dear Brother in Christ and Dear Friend.

Roberta Nichols Allen (Posthumous) – First Black Registered Nurse at Kern General Hospital – A beautiful and kind spirit.

Marie Frambrough (Posthumous) – helped form The National Council of Negro Women (NCW)-Bakersfield, and was the first President of the local chapter.

Mr. Len Edwards, (Posthumous) founder and first Director of The Bakersfield Senior Center

Mrs. Geraldine Bradley Posthumous) **she began her work as a volunteer with the local Welfare Rights Organization whose mission was to fight for the fair treatment of welfare recipients. Her efforts were recognized by the leadership of the Kern County Community Action Partnership and she was asked to serve as Director of the Senior Program of the Kern County Economic Opportunity Corporation (KCEOC). Geraldine recognized the importance of being a part of the political culture and work to gain the trust and support of state and local legislators and she was very successful! She wrote grants and proposals and was awarded funds to establish senior nutrition programs in: Delano; Buttonwillow; Wasco; Shafter; Arvin; California City; Ridgecrest; Tehachapi; Lamont; The Friendship House; Bakersfield Senior Center; MLK Senior Center; and a facility in Oildale which later became the North of the River Senior Center. Realizing that several seniors did not have transportation and some were house bound, Geraldine added a component to her nutrition program that later became a full-fledged Transportation Program and Meals on Wheels. The**

center located in MLK Community Center, was expanded, under the direction of Geraldine, to a Muliti-Purpose Senior Center that included exercise programs and activities.

Mr. Ray S. Dezember (Posthumous) He helped me get a forty million dollar line of credit for The California Gas Procurement Group (CGPG) that was later taken off the table.

Mr. Glen Hierlmeier was instrumental in getting a loan from Castle and Cook, (That was repaid from the invoices earned from our landscaping contract with Castle and Cook).

Mrs. Lillie Parker current Director of Bakersfield Senior Center, she provides the energy that fuels the continued growth and development of the center.

Letha Ora Wofford Cruise Brown (Posthumous) – My mother, who found the Lord in the Winter of Her Life who raised a family of ten without her husband in the home.

John Peterson a young man who dared to dream about the things he wanted in life, a wife, a car, a job, a house, a degree, he won.

Wayne Blake, (Leo I HAVE SOME PICTURES AND DIALOG ON TEXT MESSAGE THAT I WOULD LIKE TO INSERT HERE, AS WELL A SOME TEXT INFO FROM ANOTHER PERSON I MET ON THE TRAIN)

John Zelen A multi-talented person who cleared the system and now has a steady job, own an over the road truck, has included a son in his work and his life.

Anthony Nellums A persistent young man who has returned to driving trucks over the road, and will soon own his own fleet of trucks.

Mary Louise Randle Recently released from prison, now living in Kansas City, Mo found a job, soon to move into her own apartment.

Ralph Jennings is a multitalented man who continues to try and minister to those who are traveling the same road that he once traveled. He also participated by writing a chapter about his life.

When I started the Fresh Start Program in October 2015 I said "if we get one person to change their life, it would be a success. Now we shall induct our members into the Hall from Kenya

Erick Otiengo A young man who is the President of Pull Up From Poverty-Kenya, and continues to be an indispensable part of the success and continued growth in Kenya.

Michael Ongech (Posthumous) Educator and schoolmaster who taught and mentored hundreds of students who made a positive change in the life of others.

Josephat Moses, Founder and Director of Center for Africa Volunteers (CAV) and part owner of The International Institute For Research and Agricultural Development, LTD (IIRAD)-Kenya.

Kevin Ochuoga, (Posthumous) The first minister of the Sega church of Christ, in Sega, Kenya.

The 80 village widows of Pull Up From Poverty Kenya who take care of three hundred seventy orphans in ten separate villages in rural Kenya.

Finally, I would like to thank my God who performed the miracles that made this all possible.

CHAPTER TWENTY-TWO

HOW TO START AND HOW WE LEND MONEY

Pull Up From Poverty-America will began to make loans to co-op members on or about July 1, 2024. We will model our system used by The Grameen Bank of Bangladesh. The following steps are required to obtain a loan. We loan money to individuals who must identify with a group of four additional applicants. Again these are individual loans. In the spirit of community, if one of the five who are in the group default, the other members will not be able to obtain another loan for two years.

In Kenya where we have operated since 2007, the repayment rate is 99.3 percent, if one group member does not have the ability to make their full payment, the group join in making the payment thereby remaining eligible for higher loans.

We shall have all of the details in place after obtaining clearance to establish the institution; however, it is important to inform potential borrowers of the ground rules.

1. No credit checks
2. No contracts (because we do not sue for non-payment.
3. No co-signers.

May you remain blessed!

CHAPTER TWENTY-THREE

WE FOUND OUR FORTY ACRES

I invite you to read the account surrounding the agreement regarding the forty acres promised to freemen in 1865. The historical facts are located in Wikipedia on the google platform.

In order for you to understand the magnitude and the importance of this chapter, it is necessary to learn about the history and background of the subject and the people who were involved. The first thing we need to understand is there never was a promise of a mule on a national level. When General William T. Sherman gave some mules to some of the local freedmen because of an overabundance of pack-mules, Sherman received special files order 15 on January 16, 1865, to allot land to former slave family.

Due to this new experiment of how democracy should work, and the mixed direction from the government, General Sherman met with a group of twenty people, many of whom had been slaves for most of their lives. The blacks of Savannah, Georgia has seized this opportunity strengthen their new-found voice. They selected one spokesperson: Garrison Frazier, the 67-year-old former pastor of third African Baptist church. They met at 8:00 pm on January 12, 1865, who had purchased freedom for himself and his wife for $100,000. Fraizer consulted with the refugees as well as the other representatives. He told Sherman *"The way we can best take care of ourselves is to have land, and turn it, and till it by our own labor."* Frazier suggested that young men would serve the government in fighting the rebels, and that therefore the women, children and old men would have to work this land. Almost all of those preset agreed to their request and some land granted to the group represented and for other autonomous black communities, on the grounds that racial hatred would prevent economic advancement for black in mixed areas.

One of the first things that President Andrew Johnson did after taking office after the assassination of President Lincoln was to resigned field order 15 that returned the more than 400,000 acres of land to the former slave owners the positive effects that decedents of slave owners are still depositing in the bank. Our forty acres is in your back, side or even your front yard. The answer is land. There is 43,450 square feet of land in an acre, is 108.8 owners of 400 square feet of yard is an acre. Many very rich people all over the world are rushing to purchase land, our 40 acres is just divided up mostly into city lots and through technology that is already established in organizations like you can grow earth and selling of food locally and all over the world. We have also learned about families who own significant holdings purchased by their ancestors who moved to the urban areas like Saint Louis, Chicago, Detroit, seeking a better life but continued to pay their taxes and still own land in the south. For reasons that are as individuals as their reasons, most have no desire to sell or lease their land or farm it. To make a point, I belong to a local senior organization called, The Bakerfield Senior Center, with a membership of approximately one-hundred-forty members. In conversational interviews with two members, I learned that they had a total of twenty acres of farmland not being used for their intended purpose of producing food. We calculated that by adding a back or side-yard area of ten by forty feet, it would require us to organize one hundred and nine urban farmers to farm an acre that could be out into the supply chain starting at the local level and spread as far as the supply chain will take them. I can't speak for anybody else but there are a great number of terms and information that I did not know about or what they meant. In order for us to find their forty acres. I think it is necessary to share what I have learned or in a few cases have introduced a few phrases to explain what I am trying to say.

CIRCULAR ECONOMICS:

My short explanation is explained in this manner, if I sell it and you buy it, don't buy it outside of your circle.

Supply Chain: Sounds innocent enough, but few equate it to how goods and services are moved from one place to another. A simple example is passing large trucks on our highways, we can sometime get an idea of what it is carrying by the inscription on the truck, but er recognize that the truck is carrying something that the owner expects the end-user to buy.

Seeds innocent enough huh? Anything when planted, produced after its own kind when planted in good soil. It is true that most poor people are not involved in the beginning of the supply chain, but mostly in the end of the chain farthest from the beginning.

Where do we go from here? First, we must pray that we are willing to believe that we can make this effort work, and secondly, that we will have faith that God will be with this effort, not just in America but all over the world. We have begun to establish a supply chain from our yard to a table next door, and to tables on the other side of the world. The proceeds from the sale of this book are the seed that we are planting to get our forty acres. If any of this make sense join us at www.globalbiostimulant.com, a new site that will outline the step-by-step method to make this effort a success. Because of the magnitude of this endeavor, we cannot miss our target on the first shot.

I believe God has given us a way to improve not only life after death, and a better way of living in this life from the day that I arrived in Bakersfield on August 7, 1978; as we descended into the valley floor, I said that Bakersfield reminded me of Bethlehem, and unlike my plan to visit my mother and my sister, and play golf for three months, I knew that I would spend the remainder of my life here. Many years have passed, forty-five years and two months to be exact. On September 1st, I noticed an article in our local newspaper regarding the retooling of a refinery located on Rosedale highway to produce renewable diesel, some viewed it as a possible way to obtained jobs, but I saw the results of poor people, regardless of race ethnicity to reap the benefits of a promise made to freedmen at the end of the civil war we have started to take the necessary steps to the principles involve, to a sale food to ourselves and to participate in the supply chain needed by the bio-diesel industry staring here in Bakersfield. We began to develop this plan in the city of Sega, Kenya, and developed a relationship with a seed company that sell seeds in sixty foreign countries. And a company in America, who sale an organic bio stimulant that increases yield, and reduces irrigation needs by as much as sixty percent. There are many families that own forty acres, our plan will certainly include those who desire to participate, but our plan for urban farming will include anyone who owns a minimum of ten feet by forty feet of land. We plan to start planting in Kenya in December 2023 and in March of 2024. We are currently in the process of using trying, using, proving systems and new technology available today. We can and we will win.